NETWORKING
WITH NETWARE®
FOR
DUMMIES®

Quick Reference

by Ed Tittel, James Gaskin, and David Johnson

IDG BOOKS WORLDWIDE™

IDG Books Worldwide, Inc.
An International Data Group Company

Foster City, CA ✦ Chicago, IL ✦ Indianapolis, IN ✦ New York, NY

Networking With NetWare® For Dummies® Quick Reference

Published by
IDG Books Worldwide, Inc.
An International Data Group Company
919 E. Hillsdale Blvd.
Suite 400
Foster City, CA 94404
www.idgbooks.com (IDG Books Worldwide Web site)
www.dummies.com (Dummies Press Web site)

Library of Congress Catalog Card No.: 98-86187

ISBN: 0-7645-0306-5

Printed in the United States of America

10 9 8 7 6 5 4 3 2 1

1P/SU/QY/ZY/IN

Distributed in the United States by IDG Books Worldwide, Inc.

Distributed by Macmillan Canada for Canada; by Transworld Publishers Limited in the United Kingdom; by IDG Norge Books for Norway; by IDG Sweden Books for Sweden; by Woodslane Pty. Ltd. for Australia; by Woodslane (NZ) Ltd. for New Zealand; by Addison Wesley Longman Singapore Pte Ltd. for Singapore, Malaysia, Thailand, Indonesia and Korea; by Norma Comunicaciones S.A. for Colombia; by Intersoft for South Africa; by International Thomson Publishing for Germany, Austria and Switzerland; by Toppan Company Ltd. for Japan; by Distribuidora Cuspide for Argentina; by Livraria Cultura for Brazil; by Ediciencia S.A. for Ecuador; by Ediciones ZETA S.C.R. Ltda. for Peru; by WS Computer Publishing Corporation, Inc., for the Philippines; by Unalis Corporation for Taiwan; by Contemporanea de Ediciones for Venezuela; by Computer Book & Magazine Store for Puerto Rico; by Express Computer Distributors for the Caribbean and West Indies. Authorized Sales Agent: Anthony Rudkin Associates for the Middle East and North Africa.

For general information on IDG Books Worldwide's books in the U.S., please call our Consumer Customer Service department at 800-762-2974. For reseller information, including discounts and premium sales, please call our Reseller Customer Service department at 800-434-3422.

For information on where to purchase IDG Books Worldwide's books outside the U.S., please contact our International Sales department at 650-655-3200 or fax 650-655-3297.

For information on foreign language translations, please contact our Foreign & Subsidiary Rights department at 650-655-3021 or fax 650-655-3281.

For sales inquiries and special prices for bulk quantities, please contact our Sales department at 650-655-3200 or write to the address above.

For information on using IDG Books Worldwide's books in the classroom or for ordering examination copies, please contact our Educational Sales department at 800-434-2086 or fax 317-596-5499.

For press review copies, author interviews, or other publicity information, please contact our Public Relations department at 650-655-3000 or fax 650-655-3299.

For authorization to photocopy items for corporate, personal, or educational use, please contact Copyright Clearance Center, 222 Rosewood Drive, Danvers, MA 01923, or fax 978-750-4470.

is a trademark under exclusive license to IDG Books Worldwide, Inc., from International Data Group, Inc.

About the Authors

Ed Tittel has been a freelance writer for more than a dozen years. He's contributed to 60-plus books, including five ...*For Dummies* titles on topics that include NetWare, networking Windows NT, HTML, and XML. He's also published widely in the computer trade press, for journals from the now-defunct *Byte* Magazine to the *Web Developer's Journal* (and many points in between). Ed is a former Director of Technical Marketing for Novell, Inc., where he worked from 1988 to 1994. An adopted native of Austin, Texas, Ed has lived there for more than 20 years and has loved every minute of it. Whenever he's not busy writing or teaching, Ed enjoys cooking, playing with his new Labrador puppy, Blackie, and shooting pool. You can reach Ed via e-mail at etittel@lanw.com.

James Gaskin has written seven books on interconnecting PC networks and how they connect to the rest of the world. His most recent books include portions of *Networking With NetWare For Dummies,* 4th Edition, *IntranetWare BorderManager* and *The Complete Guide to NetWare 4.11/IntranetWare* for Sybex/Network Press, and *NetWare to Internet Gateways* and *Corporate Politics and the Internet: Connection Without Controversy* for Prentice-Hall. James is a regular contributor to *Inter@ctive Week, Network World,* and *Information Week,* where he reviews new network technologies and writes occasional features on technology. You can reach James via e-mail at james@gaskin.com.

David Johnson (also known as DJ) has worked in the networking trenches as a network administrator, manager, and trainer for eight years. Working for large corporations such as Pharmaco and GTECH, he learned his way around LAN and WAN technologies in exotic locations that range from Trinidad to the U.K. to Brazil to Warwick, Rhode Island, and back home to Austin, Texas. So far, he's contributed to 12 networking and Windows NT-related titles, which focus on certification. He's ecstatic to be writing about NetWare again! In his "spare time," DJ enjoys nothing more than a good book, a nice meal, and a bottle of outstanding Cabernet.

ABOUT IDG BOOKS WORLDWIDE

Welcome to the world of IDG Books Worldwide.

IDG Books Worldwide, Inc., is a subsidiary of International Data Group, the world's largest publisher of computer-related information and the leading global provider of information services on information technology. IDG was founded more than 25 years ago and now employs more than 8,500 people worldwide. IDG publishes more than 275 computer publications in over 75 countries (see listing below). More than 90 million people read one or more IDG publications each month.

Launched in 1990, IDG Books Worldwide is today the #1 publisher of best-selling computer books in the United States. We are proud to have received eight awards from the Computer Press Association in recognition of editorial excellence and three from *Computer Currents'* First Annual Readers' Choice Awards. Our best-selling *...For Dummies*® series has more than 50 million copies in print with translations in 38 languages. IDG Books Worldwide, through a joint venture with IDG's Hi-Tech Beijing, became the first U.S. publisher to publish a computer book in the People's Republic of China. In record time, IDG Books Worldwide has become the first choice for millions of readers around the world who want to learn how to better manage their businesses.

Our mission is simple: Every one of our books is designed to bring extra value and skill-building instructions to the reader. Our books are written by experts who understand and care about our readers. The knowledge base of our editorial staff comes from years of experience in publishing, education, and journalism — experience we use to produce books for the '90s. In short, we care about books, so we attract the best people. We devote special attention to details such as audience, interior design, use of icons, and illustrations. And because we use an efficient process of authoring, editing, and desktop publishing our books electronically, we can spend more time ensuring superior content and spend less time on the technicalities of making books.

You can count on our commitment to deliver high-quality books at competitive prices on topics you want to read about. At IDG Books Worldwide, we continue in the IDG tradition of delivering quality for more than 25 years. You'll find no better book on a subject than one from IDG Books Worldwide.

IDG BOOKS
WORLDWIDE

John Kilcullen
CEO
IDG Books Worldwide, Inc.

Steven Berkowitz
President and Publisher
IDG Books Worldwide, Inc.

Eighth Annual
Computer Press
Awards ≥1992

IX
WINNER

Ninth Annual
Computer Press
Awards ≥1993

WINNER

Tenth Annual
Computer Press
Awards ≥1994

XI
WINNER

Eleventh Annual
Computer Press
Awards ≥1995

Authors' Acknowledgments

As always, we have more people to thank than we have room for on this page. For that reason, we'd like to thank everyone who worked on this project that we don't mention by name. As you know, we couldn't have done it without you, even if your name isn't featured here. Thanks!!

Ed Tittel: To begin with, I'd like to thank my co-authors, David (DJ) Johnson and James Gaskin. Without their contributions, this book could never have happened. Next, I'd like to thank my long-suffering agent, Carole McClendon, and her agency, Waterside Productions, for their excellent representation over the years. I'd also like to thank the IDG editorial staff, including Ellen Camm, who's moved on to another role but who brokered this job for us, Mike Kelly, Colleen Williams, and Colleen Rainsberger. I'd also like to thank my mom, again, for cultivating a lifelong interest in learning and language that has always stood me in good stead. Finally, I'd like to thank Tressa, David Jules, Summer Dawn, and the fabulous Charlene for their time, energy, and love, and for helping me find meaning in life beyond the keyboard. Thanks to one and all!

James Gaskin: First, I appreciate my lovely wife Wendy, handsome son Alex, and darling daughter Laura for letting me steal time from them to write this book. I always promise not to sneak off and work in the evenings or on weekends, but I do anyway. Sorry. Working with Ed over the years as we cross paths at NetWorld+InterOp and the like has been a pleasure, and being asked to become an official ...For Dummies author is a great honor, improved only by working with DJ as the other author. Many Novell people have helped me over the years, and special thanks go to Jason Werner, Henry Sprafkin, Brian Faustyn, Gordon Evans, Michael Simpson, and last, but not least, the wonderful Katrina Larson. Thanks to you all for keeping me up to date.

David "DJ" Johnson: Well, first off, I'd like to thank my co-author, Ed Tittel, for giving me the opportunity to move back home and pursue a life I never dreamed existed. I'd also like to thank my other co-author, James Gaskin, for stepping up when we needed him most. James, you are a consummate professional and working with you has been a pleasure. As always, thanks to the staff at LANWrights and particularly Mary Burmeister. Thanks for your hard work on this book. Finally, I'd like to thank my best friend and confidant, Ahnon, for reminding me what life is really about.

All of us would like to thank the staff at IDG Books Worldwide, particularly Colleen Williams, our project editor, and William Barton, Kathleen Dobie, and Stephanie Koutek, our copy editors. We'd also like to thank Mike Kelly for his direction as we started this project and Ellen Camm who, as Ed mentioned, has moved on to greener pastures but started us rolling along. Finally, we'd like to thank all the other editorial and production folk that work behind the scenes. We know you're back there guys; thanks for the hard work!

Please feel free to contact any of us, care of IDG Books Worldwide, 919 E. Hillsdale Blvd., Suite 400, Foster City, CA 94404.

Publisher's Acknowledgments

We're proud of this book; please register your comments through our IDG Books Worldwide Online Registration Form located at: http://my2cents.dummies.com.

Some of the people who helped bring this book to market include the following:

Acquisitions, Editorial, and Media Development

Project Editor: Colleen Williams

Acquisitions Editor: Michael Kelly

Copy Editors: William A. Barton, Kathleen Dobie, and Stephanie Koutek

Technical Editor: Mary T. Madden

Editorial Manager: Leah P. Cameron

Editorial Assistant: Donna Love

Production

Project Coordinator: E. Shawn Aylsworth

Layout and Graphics: Lou Boudreau, Angela F. Hunckler, Brent Savage, Drew R. Moore, Kate Snell

Proofreaders: Christine Berman, Kelli Botta, Melissa D. Buddendeck, Nancy Price, Janet M. Withers

Indexer: Sharon Hilgenberg

General and Administrative

IDG Books Worldwide, Inc.: John Kilcullen, CEO; Steven Berkowitz, President and Publisher

IDG Books Technology Publishing: Brenda McLaughlin, Senior Vice President and Group Publisher

Dummies Technology Press and Dummies Editorial: Diane Graves Steele, Vice President and Associate Publisher; Mary Bednarek, Director of Acquisitions and Product Development; Kristin A. Cocks, Editorial Director

Dummies Trade Press: Kathleen A. Welton, Vice President and Publisher; Kevin Thornton, Acquisitions Manager

IDG Books Production for Dummies Press: Michael R. Britton, Vice President of Production and Creative Services; Beth Jenkins Roberts, Production Director; Cindy L. Phipps, Manager of Project Coordination, Production Proofreading, and Indexing; Kathie S. Schutte, Supervisor of Page Layout; Shelley Lea, Supervisor of Graphics and Design; Debbie J. Gates, Production Systems Specialist; Robert Springer, Supervisor of Proofreading; Debbie Stailey, Special Projects Coordinator; Tony Augsburger, Supervisor of Reprints and Bluelines

Dummies Packaging and Book Design: Robin Seaman, Creative Director; Jocelyn Kelaita, Product Packaging Coordinator; Kavish + Kavish, Cover Design

◆

The publisher would like to give special thanks to Patrick J. McGovern, without whom this book would not have been possible.

◆

Table of Contents

How to Use This Book

Networking With NetWare For Dummies Quick Reference gives you the short, quick answer to the most common NetWare questions for the most common versions of NetWare. No one can remember every command for every version of NetWare, but you can certainly look up the command that you need right here.

No, you don't find the entire story and command set of all NetWare versions in this slim but action-packed book. But if you believe in the old 80–20 rule (that 20 percent of the commands perform 80 percent of the work), you're sure to find this book a great value.

We doubt that you're going read this book cover to cover sequentially, although you can if you really want to. Most often, however, you're going to start immediately searching for something particular. That's why the Table of Contents and Index are set up the way we have them — to help you find what you need quickly and get right back to your network.

How This Book Is Organized

We organize *Networking With NetWare For Dummies Quick Reference* into seven major parts. At the end you find a couple of helpful appendixes and a Glossary for any words about which you're still curious, plus the Index to help you find subjects quickly. The following list describes these seven parts:

✦ *Part I, "Getting to Know NetWare,"* explains where NetWare came from, why it's the way it is, and some of the reasons that NetWare works so well for so many companies around the world. We explain each version of the program, from NetWare 3.*x* through NetWare 5, along with some extras from Novell that can expand your network. Because you may need to retrain some executive management members now and then, we describe some of the benefits of local and wide area networks, particularly those that NetWare powers, in simple terms that every manager can understand.

✦ *Part II, "Installing and Configuring NetWare,"* covers how to prepare the system that's to become your server, how to install various versions of NetWare on that server, and what to verify after you finish installation. Of course, an installed network isn't a finished network, so we also cover the guts of network administration in this part. We help you set up the file system, add some users, get your Directory services going, add some security, and even communicate with the rest of the world via the Internet.

✦ *Part III, "The Major NetWare Utilities and Tools,"* dives head-first into the applications that you use to nudge NetWare in the direction you need to support your particular network situation. Some of these utilities we also mention in Part II for initial network configuration, but some (such as the utilities that your users see) are new to this part.

✦ *Part IV, "NetWare Tools, Commands, and Minor Utilities,"* presents command-line utilities and applications, including a few that you don't need often but that can save your bacon every few months. Then we examine the newer graphical utilities, having your mouse manage your NetWare network for a change.

✦ *Part V, "Integrating NetWare and Windows NT,"* makes peacefully combining NetWare and Windows NT a simple matter for your network, even if Microsoft can't admit that such a thing is possible. Microsoft offers some tools, but those from Novell are almost always better. You're probably going to need to mix both operating systems in your network. If you must migrate some users from NetWare to Windows NT or vice versa, we give you a head start for that project as well.

✦ *Part VI, "Common Administrative Tasks,"* covers most of the typical day's management and control functions, as well as some unusual situations necessary for certain network situations, such as connecting to remote systems. We discuss Web-server details, backups, printer secrets, tricks and life-savers, and typical user-management tasks in this part and describe them all in plenty of detail so that you or your helpers can make things work smoothly.

✦ *Part VII, "Making the NetWare-to-Internet Connection,"* shows you how to add TCP/IP to NetWare and how to configure network settings and protocols with INETCFG. This part outlines IP addressing basics and configuring TCP/IP.

✦ *Appendix A, "How to Get Help When You Need It Most,"* is a quick reference on how to get along with technical support people. It offers suggestions on getting your information organized so that you don't waste your money and your technical support person's time. This appendix also intro-duces different sources for information that you can use to get quick answers.

✦ *Appendix B, "NetWare Information Online,"* points you to resources you can use online to get the answers you need.

✦ *The glossary of terms, "Techie Talk,"* includes all the new NetWare or networking-oriented terms that you may not have run into in polite conversation. Use this as a "word-a-day" course or just refer to it as necessary. Either way, the terms and definitions are here waiting for you whenever you need them.

Conventions Used in This Book

Commands, utility names, and parameters (which you can read about in Part IV) appear `in this typeface`. See how easy that was? For example:

`LOAD MONITOR`

Not so hard, is it? (The only exception is if we're telling you to type them directly onscreen, in which case they appear in **bold** type.)

Remember to press the Enter key after every command, even if we don't remember to remind you.

`This is an on-screen message.`

See? This stuff is all pretty clear, and soon, NetWare is going to be clear to you as well.

Need More Information?

No single book (and between we three authors, we've written some big ones) can completely cover a topic as large as NetWare. You quickly pick up on how to type HELP at the colon prompt on the server console, however, and the Novell documentation is getting almost helpful in sections.

Don't forget the Internet as a resource. Novell's Web sites (at www.novell.com and www.support.novell.com) are doing a good job getting valuable, if at times arcane, information out to the public.

Most of all, remember that your NetWare dealers and associated consultants can help. Don't call them for the easy stuff (and more than you realize is the easy stuff — which we cover in this book), but don't lose their number, either.

Icons Used in This Book

Look at the margins — see strange little cartoons? You soon discover that these little pictures, known as icons, help you pick out something important about NetWare — we promise.

You cut time and/or aggravation by following one of these pro-tested Tips.

The pros pick up some of these tricks through trial and error, so learn from their mistakes and pay attention whenever you see this Warning sign.

You find information on the quickest way to accomplish something, under normal circumstances, if you see this icon.

This icon points to features that may not act as you expect.

This icon flags you to information that's new and special to NetWare 5.

Getting to Know NetWare

Because every network grows and, of course, you're constantly upgrading it with new versions of your operating software, Part I explains the differences between the versions of NetWare, as well as where each version provides the best benefits. You also discover ways to increase your network's ROI — that is, *R*eturn *O*n *I*nvestment, a fancy slogan that accountants use for how much bang you get for your buck — and even some ways that you can boost your network budget.

In this part . . .

- ✔ **Understanding the foundations of NetWare**
- ✔ **Decoding the features of each NetWare version**
- ✔ **Examining complementary products from Novell**
- ✔ **Covering ways that NetWare can help your company**

What Is NetWare?

NetWare is a "network-specific" operating system, in contrast to "general-purpose" operating systems such as Windows 95, 98, NT, and Unix, among others.

But what exactly *is* the difference between network-specific and general-purpose operating systems? The following list describes the purpose of each type of system:

✦ Network-specific operating systems, such as NetWare, by design provide file, print, security, messaging, and management services to clients across a network.

✦ General-purpose operating systems, such as Windows, Unix, DOS, and even OS/2, focus more on providing application services, primarily for the system that's running the operating system.

Yes, the lines get blurry at times. Microsoft touts Windows NT as a network server on one hand, while saying that it's better than NetWare because it also supports applications. Contrary to what you might hear from the crew in Redmond, NetWare does run applications at the server, and now NetWare 5 even runs graphical applications at the server, which puts it on par with Windows NT for ease of use and just plain beauty.

Yet the focus of NetWare and those applications running on the server is to provide services to clients. Running local applications takes up plenty of program code in the operating system and lots of machine resources like CPU time. Stripping out everything but network services and necessary support for network applications means that the file server runs faster and jumps higher. An example of this approach is realized with Unix systems that are optimized as network servers. Like a Unix system, NetWare engineers have stripped out the code those systems use to run applications, making the servers real speed demons.

NetWare and Networking

Novell's first attempt at a product was designed to leverage the power of a PC running the CP/M operating system (a pre-DOS OS) with one CPU over multiple dumb terminals. Flowing with the tide, Novell programmers took an early PC from IBM and decided that adding some intelligence at the end of the network wire could be a good approach. One advantage of this approach was longevity.

In the early 1980s, Novell Data Systems was folded into Novell, Inc. A group of outside contractors known as Superset, led by Drew Major, wrote the early operating system to enable NetWare to handle DOS clients and hasn't looked back since.

Why NetWare is NetWare

Novell programmers did many things that were opposite conventional wisdom. At the time, their ideas were considered strange, but now, much of the world agrees with the basic NetWare philosophy.

Two elements made NetWare stand out, as follows:

✦ NetWare isn't built on DOS or any part of DOS. Nor is it built on Unix or any other general-purpose operating system. It's a dedicated and newly developed network operating system.

✦ File service has always been the top priority for NetWare servers. After all, what good are shared files if you have to wait for them? The following two big breakthroughs put file performance on the fast track at Novell:

• **Elevator Seeking.** When files are written to a hard disk, they are stored almost randomly across the media. Back when disks were larger than a pack of cards, you could hear the heads jerking back and forth as they were accessing files. Every change of direction the heads make wastes time, so Novell engineers designed NetWare to access the server's disk in the same way that an elevator accesses floors — not first come, first served, but rather serving each request in the order it appears while moving in the direction that the disk heads are already going. When the heads reach the end of the disk, they reverse direction and fulfill the remaining requests. This "elevator" style means less time wasted and faster file service.

• **Caching.** File caching simply means keeping copies of recently accessed files in the system's RAM after clients are through using them. RAM access is many times faster than disk access, so clients receive popular files faster from the cache than they could from the disk. Keeping the disk directories in memory instead of reading the file from the disk also means that you can find file locations much more quickly than you can without caching.

NetWare focuses on *client service* first and everything else second.

NetWare embraces everyone

In the early days of PC networking, most NetWare competitors were selling network operating systems to spur sales of network cards or file servers.

Novell took the opposite approach and wrote software to support every network card on the market. Only NetWare, for example, provided network connections for such machines as the TI PC, DEC Rainbow, or the Victor 9000 (IBM almost-clones).

This idea of providing software for other company's network cards became known as *co-opetition*, a term that Novell CEO Ray Noorda coined. The overriding Novell philosophy was that a rising tide raises all the boats at the dock. In other words, the more networking systems that were in existence, the more business all network vendors could enjoy.

Novell got away from that philosophy for a time, but new CEO Eric Schmidt seems to understand the value of working with every company in the market. One thing for sure is that Novell is doing much more to help integrate and manage Windows 95/98/NT systems with NetWare servers than Microsoft is doing to cooperate with NetWare.

Novell's greatest networking achievement — Directory Services

Directory services may sound pretty dull and boring to your average office worker, but they really aren't. Imagine NDS (*Novell Directory Services*) as the bouncer at a fancy club, for example, allowing authorized guests in, keeping riff-raff out, and directing some guests to private party rooms. Pretty fun image with all that dancing and excitement, huh? Well, that's exactly what NDS does on your server . . . but without the dancing, of course.

A *Directory* (capital D) is a special type of database that tracks network objects and resources, as well as the security levels of each of those network devices and users. This Directory database holds all the information for NDS, and you access it primarily through the NetWare Administrator graphical utility. A *directory* (small *d*), on the other hand, is simply a file-system structure for coordinating files that you store together. If you see *directory* (small *d*), think file structure; if you see *Directory* (big *D*), think NDS and the bouncer.

NDS is one of Novell's great achievements, and the company has reason to be proud of its work. After all, wouldn't you like to have one central clearinghouse in your company that controls every employee's access to other employees as well as to company equipment and resources, making the same information available to everyone? That's what NDS does for your network. NetWare and NDS can organize your network while telling you exactly where everything and everyone is at all times.

NetWare/IntranetWare Makes and Models, Choices and Options

A company that started in 1979 is likely to have quite a few products and versions to discuss, and Novell is no different.

Practically speaking, few companies still use NetWare 2.*x* software, at least in the United States. NetWare v3.0 first shipped in 1989; 18 months later, with v3.11, NetWare finally had the full TCP/IP support that it promised to provide in v3.0. (You know how software slips.) So in the following sections, we focus on NetWare 3.*x* and up. After that, we also take a look at some of Novell's other products: BorderManager, GroupWise, and ManageWise.

NetWare 3.x

As the first network operating system to fully exploit a 32-bit CPU (80386), NetWare 3.*x* offered the level of performance and stability that large corporate networks need. Even today, hundreds of thousands of NetWare 3.*x* servers chug merrily along.

The features of NetWare 3.*x* are as follows:

- ✦ The 32-bit processor provides plenty of horsepower.

- ✦ *NetWare Loadable Modules* (NLMs) make their appearance, providing ways for third parties to extend NetWare's power.

- ✦ Built-in support for many protocols (including routing), like IPX, TCP/IP, AppleTalk, and even a subset of SNA.

- ✦ Increased server management and control flexibility, including easy remote server administration.

The increased demands on today's networks daily push more companies to upgrade. If your company still uses multiple 3.*x* servers, you may want to start the budget process for an upgrade.

NetWare 4.x

NetWare 4 debuted in March 1993, with a flashy presentation at the InterOp trade show. A thousand and one Compaq systems, tied into one network, started out first as 1,000 workstations and 1 server and then — presto-chango! — they became 1,000 servers managed by a single workstation. NDS debuted at that demonstration, and in fact, such a feat became possible only through the use of NDS.

Again, the 4.11 release of NetWare really delivered the promised goods, although 4.1 had its share of success. The following features cover the entire NetWare 4.x gamut:

+ Additive user licenses enable you to build a 60-user network by adding a 50-user license and a 10-user license instead of needing to buy the 100-user license. Denominations include 5-, 10-, 25-, 50-, 100-, 250-, 500-, and 1,000-user versions.

+ NDS enables administrators to manage the entire network as one entity, not as a dozen individual servers, each with its own set of users and security controls. One Directory now handles one network, no matter how large it is.

+ TCP/IP support, even for NetWare client to NetWare server communications, starts the move away from Novell's reliance on its own proprietary IPX protocol.

+ Built-in disk compression supports as much as three or four times as many files as disk size indicates. Many users find the savings for disk space alone pays for their upgrade.

+ The CD-ROM-based installation, including CD-ROM NetWare drivers that enable a server to offer a CD-ROM disk as a NetWare volume usable by all NetWare clients.

+ Graphical utilities manage users, printers, servers, and security access for each item.

+ File system supports long filenames from DOS, Windows 95/98/ NT, OS/2, Macintosh, and NFS (Network File System) Unix files.

NetWare 4.x really upped the ante, taking the hardware that's available (Pentium chips and cheaper memory) to new heights of user count, functionality, and ease of management.

IntranetWare

IntranetWare was the creation of the Novell executive team before the arrival of Eric Schmidt from Sun Microsystems. While their intentions were good, their execution of differentiating various flavors of NetWare 4.x were poor.

Put simply, IntranetWare is NetWare 4.11 with some extra "stuff" using Internet technologies. Though priced the same as NetWare 4.11, IntranetWare included the following extra features:

+ **NetWare/IP:** Allows NetWare clients to communicate with NetWare servers using TCP/IP rather than IPX/SPX.

✦ **NetWare/FLeX/IP:** Bi-directional print services between Unix and NetWare, along with file transfer goodies, including an FTP server for NetWare.

✦ **NetWare Web Server 2.5:**. A fast but incomplete Web server running on the NetWare 4.11 and IntranetWare server. It was planned to be only in IntranetWare, but Novell executives made the IntranetWare decision too late to pull the Web server off the NetWare 4.11 installation CD-ROM.

✦ **NetWare IPX-to-IP Gateway:** Allows NetWare Windows clients to communicate over IPX to the NetWare server, then convert the protocol to TCP/IP for the Internet. Software fools the Internet applications, such as Web browsers, into believing there is TCP/IP on the client, even though there isn't.

✦ **TCP/IP address management services:** Utilities to handle TCP/IP network address chores, such as assigning IP addresses and connecting with Internet name servers.

✦ **NAT (Network Address Translation):** Converts the internal TCP/IP addresses used to a different IP network address when packets leave the network. Great for security, because it hides the real addresses of your network devices, and even greater for combining disparate networks forced to work together due to company reorganizations or mergers.

✦ **Netscape Navigator:** The best Web client software available comes on the NetWare CD-ROM for all Windows clients in your network.

The good news is that NetWare 4.11/IntranetWare moved NetWare into position as a complete Internet network operating system, filling in all the gaps NetWare 4.10 had left. For instance, the Novell Web Server was available before the NetWare IPX-to-IP Gateway was ready, meaning you could use NetWare as a Web server on the Internet, but none of your local NetWare clients could see the Web part of the server. IntranetWare fixed that, and suddenly NetWare servers and clients became full Internet denizens for the first time.

Wait, you say! The most important piece is missing — the NetWare Web server. True, IntranetWare included Novell's first Web server, but so did NetWare 4.11. Why? Novell decided on the IntranetWare feature package too late to pull the Web server out of NetWare 4.11, so the Web server shipped with the "base" NetWare package even though it should have gone out only in the IntranetWare box.

NetWare 5

The latest and greatest NetWare version takes NetWare from its previous status as a local-area network system to a global network system. Engineers reworked NetWare to make it as Internet

compatible as possible. They also increased its manageability,
security, and performance by changing plenty of technical stuff
under the hood. The result? NetWare 5!

Novell executives reapportioned the Internet pieces of NetWare
4.11 and IntranetWare between NetWare 5 and BorderManager
(discussed in the "Other Novell Goodies" section). Essentially, the
Internet connection pieces are still in NetWare, but the security
and performance-enhancing connection parts were moved to
BorderManager. Following is a short list of NetWare 5 improvements:

✦ Native TCP/IP links between clients and servers as the default,
   with IPX as the second choice.

✦ Improved memory management, including virtual memory
   (spooling the least-used RAM portions out to disk) to increase
   memory size and stability.

✦ Complete GUI server installation and control.

✦ Java support throughout the NetWare server, including on the
   server itself high-performance Java Virtual Machine software
   that supports any Java application.

✦ Enhancements to NDS, enabling more control for submanagers
   and easier ways for users to connect.

✦ Netscape's FastTrack Web server, free in every box.

✦ Support for huge volumes and file sizes and the capability to
   mount large (up into the terabyte range) disk volumes in
   seconds rather than in minutes.

More features are available. Just be assured that NetWare 5 delivers
pretty well on the prerelease hype, so you don't need to wait until
NetWare v5.11 to get all the pieces necessary for a stout network.

Other Novell Goodies

While NetWare is Novell's shining jewel, a number of other applications are available from Novell that enhance your network. The
following sections discuss some of these applications and their uses.

BorderManager

BorderManager is a set of security, management, and performance
applications that enhances your NetWare-to-Internet connections.

BorderManager includes enhanced network security with these
features:

✦ **Firewall:** Blocks packets coming into your network from outside,
   and even controls which packets can leave your network.

✦ **IP-IP Gateway:** Adds a way to control non-NetWare clients running TCP/IP, such as Macintosh and Unix systems, on your physical network. Most of the NetWare controls affecting Internet connections apply to non-NetWare clients with the new functions of the IP-IP Gateway.

✦ **NAT:** *N*etwork *A*ddress *T*ranslation (NAT) is now in BorderManager for the additional security it offers from outsiders trying to get into your network.

Another huge addition to BorderManager is Web caching, also sold separately as FastCache. Novell took its expertise in file caching for local networks and applied it to the Internet, speeding performance tenfold for internal NetWare clients looking at the Internet, and for caching the contents of internal Web servers to speed outsider access to that information. Novell has a right to be proud of this technology, because FastCache can handle thousands of Web server hits per second. Yes, per second!

One BorderManager server, running either on an existing server or a dedicated NetWare server, can service the Internet needs for an entire network. (BorderManager includes a two-user NetWare runtime allowing it to operate on its own server.) The tools that you need for each network still come in NetWare 5, whereas the tools to control and protect the enterprise network are in BorderManager.

GroupWise

GroupWise is another application that doesn't come in the NetWare box but greatly enhances your network. Much more than just an e-mail program, GroupWise includes a universal in-box, task lists, schedules that you can share among the group, shared calendars, and links to Internet e-mail servers through a gateway. NetWare v4.11 for Small Business, a complete network system for up to 25 users, includes GroupWise. Unfortunately, GroupWise is an extra purchase item for all other NetWare configurations.

ManageWise

Being clever, you probably figure that *ManageWise* does for network management and control what GroupWise does for communication. After your network grows past 3 servers and 60 users, you need help — either in software or peopleware. Using ManageWise is cheaper than hiring another network technician and the program never takes long breaks or vacations. Check it out.

What Can NetWare/IntranetWare Do For You?

If you're new to NetWare, you may wonder what all this fuss is about. Even if you've used NetWare since the early days, however, you regularly must resell your management on all the advantages that your network provides. Review the next few sections as you're preparing the report for your boss on why you need all these gizmos.

Local Area Network (LAN) benefits

Using a LAN offers several benefits over stand-alone workstations. The following list offers a pretty good rundown of these benefits:

✦ **Communication.** Anyone on the LAN can communicate with anyone else on the LAN. Believe it or not, this setup works even better than gossiping over the water cooler.

✦ **Security.** Not everyone in the company can be privy to all the information that some people in the company must share. Leaving the payroll program on a single computer may seem safer than putting it on the network, but NetWare actually adds protection in several different ways — for example, requiring a password and providing access at only certain times of day — and NetWare can even tie access to a particular computer if your accounting manager is truly paranoid.

✦ **Safety.** Raise your hand if you ever did a full system backup to a 3-foot pile of floppy disks. Thought so. Most users never back up their personal systems, no matter how fervently they promised to do so the last time that they deleted the wrong file. NetWare can automatically back up data on the server under the watchful eye of system administrators. The cost of losing one critical batch of invoices alone can pay for your network. You're better off safe than, well, you know.

✦ **Savings.** Almost all software today has an option for network installation. By using NetWare's license utility (in NetWare v4.11 and 5), you can legally provide only the number of software copies necessary for your users. Why buy 100 copies of software for 100 users if only 25 users need the program at one time? Managers love this argument. They also love to hear that you can share one expensive color laser printer among everyone or restrict access to only those users you authorize for its use.

Wide Area Network (WAN) benefits

Using a WAN also provides several benefits. The following list gives an account of those benefits:

✦ **Communications.** Out of sight is not out of mind if you have NetWare to link offices. By using NetWare's built-in routing, along with some long-distance lines, any remote network can become part of the corporate network. Advances in the BorderManager software enable you to link remote networks securely while using your existing Internet connection, saving the cost of long-distance lines between offices.

✦ **Security.** Sharing sensitive data between offices normally means sending that information from a secured area, such as a headquarters, to an unsecured area, such as a district office. Avoid that problem by using NetWare's security and directory services to link all your offices. You can share files among offices while maintaining security.

✦ **Savings.** No one thinks about how much money you may spend sending paper via overnight business package services or how many long-distance fax calls people make between branches. If your remote offices are all on the same network, the need for package delivery and faxes disappears almost completely. The savings, however, get bigger and bigger.

Your network and the Internet

Unless you've been searching the Borneo jungle for ants the last few years, you know that every company needs Internet access. The barrier to becoming a "real" business is lack of an Internet presence — which you need both to reach your customers and for your customers to reach you.

Think that you have an argument to avoid using the Internet? Check out the following points and counterpoints:

✦ **Think that your company can't afford the huge expense of getting on the Internet or risk the security problems that it entails?**

You're not alone; many companies, especially those too small to have dedicated computer technology departments, worry about these points. NetWare, however, enables you to skip both those potential pitfalls.

✦ **Don't think that you have the right software for Internet connections?**

Every NetWare v4.11, IntranetWare, and NetWare 5 PC client has all the software that you need for Internet connections. It comes right along with the NetWare client files.

◆ **You prefer to manage a single Internet access point for security reasons?**

BorderManager provides an IPX-to-IP gateway that enables all authorized users to reach the Internet.

Every NetWare v4.11, IntranetWare, and NetWare 5 PC client also gets a copy of Netscape Navigator, arguably the best Web browser available.

Microsoft's Internet Explorer works perfectly well with NetWare, but your browser works considerably better if you set up one NetWare server to run the NetWare cache software, either from the BorderManager suite or just by using the FastCache software itself.

Part II

Installing and Configuring NetWare

This part of the book describes the process for installing NetWare, the system preparation before installation, and the critical first steps in establishing your network. We cover the version differences, and you'll notice the standard installation process gets easier as you head higher up the version numbers. We also cover the basics of IntranetWare.

Experience with Windows 95/98/NT installation won't help much, so don't try to apply those skills here. Although, experience with Unix will help you appreciate how much easier NetWare is to install and get started.

Do not start your installation in the middle of a workday with everyone watching over your shoulder. NetWare installation is pretty quick, but leave yourself time to rework the installation once or twice if necessary. No sense in putting extra pressure on yourself by inviting others to watch.

In this part...

✔ **Preparing server hardware**

✔ **Performing the installation**

✔ **Checking installation details afterward**

✔ **Getting your network configured for users and groups**

✔ **Preparing for NDS**

✔ **Securing your network with the basics**

✔ **Embracing TCP/IP**

Installing NetWare

NetWare installation details improved drastically between NetWare
3.*x* and NetWare 5, but the basic process is much the same. The
server machine must boot reliably under DOS, have functioning
CD-ROM drivers — if you plan to use the CD-ROM installation
method (recommended) — and have plenty of memory and disk
space. Room for more memory and disk space is strongly advised,
because networks almost always grow rather than shrink —
additional RAM and disk space are always welcome!

Before you begin your installation, be sure to have the following:

✦ All NetWare disks and documentation

✦ All server disks, drivers, and documentation

✦ CD-ROM information and drivers

✦ DOS disks for disk partition operations

✦ Network interface card drivers and documentation

✦ Directory Service tree and organization information for
   NetWare versions 4.*x*, 5, and IntranetWare

✦ Network protocol details, such as TCP/IP addresses and IPX
   network numbers

Preparing the server

Do not buy the cheapest possible system for your server. If
anything, go overboard on buying a server with:

✦ A large power supply (based on your hardware documentation)

✦ Plenty of room for extra RAM

✦ Plenty of room for extra disks

✦ A fast network interface card with drivers for use in a server

✦ A case large enough to get your hands inside comfortably

✦ A battery backup system

This list covers the basic server, which is fine for a workgroup or
department server, but not stout enough for a large group of users.
If budget permits, add the following to your wish list:

✦ Redundant power supplies

✦ Two or more fans to keep the server cool

✦ RAID (Redundant Array of Independent Disks) for your server
   disk storage

Adding to your server can be very beneficial. Spending a few more dollars up front often means the difference between a server that stays up and running seemingly forever and one that crashes and drags the network down with it. Buying fans to keep your server cool is important because if the power supply burns out you'll have to replace it. (As a word of caution: If you have to replace your power supply, it's better to do it after hours, rather than working on a broken server when the payroll department is trying unsuccessfully to print checks.) More RAM and disk space means your network keeps up with growth rather than being swamped by success. RAID disks, depending on the model, can have disks added or replaced without downing the server, which means more uptime.

Depending on the model, you can add or replace RAID disks without making the server go down.

One critical piece of equipment, not part of the server and there-fore easily overlooked, is the battery backup. No matter what else you forget, don't forget this. A battery backup saves you if power in the building stops for a few seconds, or power gradually loses strength now and then.

A different battery backup model, typically called a UPS (Uninterruptible Power Supply), keeps steady voltage in case of power failure or brownout. Watching the server stop while the lights dim is no fun, and can lead to damaged data files and scrambled application configuration files.

Preinstallation checklist

The following is a list of things to check before you install NetWare:

✦ **Verify that your server boots properly under DOS:** If your server just came from the dealer, go through and REMark out all the high memory driver (EMM386.EXE and the like) references in CONFIG.SYS and AUTOEXEC.BAT by editing the files and putting REM at the first of each line. Yes, doing this means that your CD-ROM drivers now load in the lower 640K of DOS, limiting your available memory for applications, but that won't matter. Once NetWare starts, all the physical memory is controlled by NetWare's own memory management software, not the less-competent versions used by DOS and Windows 95/98.

✦ **Verify that your network card is working properly:** Use the diagnostics program that comes on the drivers disk with your network card. (If your network interface card is so cheap that it didn't come with a drivers disk, take it back to your dealer and get a name-brand card certified for use in a NetWare server.) The performance of the server network card affects the performance of your entire network, so buy the best card you can afford. Show this paragraph to your boss if money is tight and you need some support for your budget request.

✦ **Verify network client access if you're connecting to another server for installation software:** It's actually faster to load the operating system across the network than from the server's own CD-ROM drive. Why? NetWare file caching on the server hosting the NetWare installation files improves file read performance for the server being installed. If you're doing a network installation, verify your NetWare client software is up and running under DOS.

✦ **Partition and format your disk(s) with a small DOS partition on the primary disk:** NetWare boots with DOS, but just for a little while until DOS loads the NetWare operating system and gets pushed out of the way. All the NetWare drivers and utility files that configure the NetWare operating system on this server must fit into the DOS partition on the hard disk, along with any DOS diagnostic utilities you wish to use. NetWare 3.*x* recommends 15MB of DOS partition space (but we think 20MB is safer), NetWare 4.*x* asks for that or more (depending on circumstances), and NetWare 5 asks for 50MB of space. Because hard disks are now relatively cheap, make your partition 50MB and don't worry about the "wasted" space. Leave the rest of the disk(s) alone; NetWare handles them during installation.

✦ **Format the DOS partition and load enough DOS drivers to get your CD-ROM disk working:** The DOS partition, small as it is, must be bootable. Part of that boot process is getting your CD-ROM drive working. Yes, you can leave that up to NetWare later, but then you won't be able to access the CD-ROM drive directly, which is handy for initial installation, and also for installing new software.

✦ **Make a boot diskette that includes the CD-ROM drivers:** Installations often require two or three passes to get things exactly right, and a bootable DOS diskette with appropriate drivers will make life much easier. If you're doing installation from another NetWare server across the network, make sure the necessary NetWare client files are on this diskette as well. This time-saver isn't mandatory, but it's strongly recommended.

A simple NetWare installation, step-by-step

Gather your configured server-to-be along with your NetWare disks and the documentation, and get comfortable. It's time to install NetWare:

1. Reboot the system to verify that no memory managers are loaded.

2. Verify that the CD-ROM drivers are loaded by trying the drive.

3. Put the NetWare CD into the CD-ROM drive.

4. Type **INSTALL** at the CD-ROM drive prompt.

5. Choose a language for NetWare to use on this server.

6. Choose NetWare Server Installation.

7. Choose Simple installation of a single NetWare server.

8. Name your new NetWare server.

   NetWare server names can be 2 to 47 characters and should be short, unique, and easily recognized — for example, ACCTSRV1. Certain characters are not allowed in server names, such as spaces, *, +, , /, \, :, and =.

9. Let NetWare find and display the disk driver information — make changes only if necessary.

10. Let NetWare find and display the network driver information, and choose your client-to-server protocol when requested to do so.

11. Feed the NetWare License Diskette into the floppy drive when requested.

12. Install NetWare Directory Services, providing an Administrator password when asked, and the tree and organization information, if applicable. For a more complex network, skip ahead to "Preparing for NetWare Directory Services" later in this section.

13. Wait for NetWare to finish copying files from the CD-ROM to the server hard disk.

14. Turn down the chance to install more products (you can come back later for this).

15. Reboot your server to complete the installation.

NetWare 5 is even easier to install, because NetWare makes more of the choices for you, and provides a good-looking graphical interface. The new installation interface doesn't provide more information or make life appreciably easier, but it does look different.

NetWare 3.*x* installation is a bit more difficult, because you must provide more information during the process. Type **SETUP** rather than INSTALL on the CD-ROM or floppy disks. If you stick to the disk and network components listed in the NetWare manual, however, NetWare 3.*x* will automatically find and configure just about everything for you. Just remember to march through each option on the Installation Options menu and you'll be fine.

Post-installation checklist

When you reboot the server at the end of an installation, several important things happen automatically and you should verify that they do happen:

- ✦ The server boots DOS without memory managers.
- ✦ The AUTOEXEC.BAT file calls the NetWare SERVER program from the \NWSERVER directory.
- ✦ NetWare loads as software module after module whizzes by too quickly to read.
- ✦ The NetWare console shows the colon prompt along with the name of the NetWare server.
- ✦ Other NetWare servers are capable of seeing the new server and vice versa (type **DISPLAY SERVERS** at the console prompt to view all the servers in the network).

Of course, your NetWare clients must be able to see the new server, log in, and use the network resources of the new server. Part III goes into the client part of NetWare in detail.

Making NetWare Work for You

Is this like multilevel marketing, where you get money by convincing your network to work for you? Not directly, but the more efficient and organized your network, the less hectic your day.

A network that provides what users need to perform their jobs on a daily basis is a network that works for you and your users. If users constantly have to ask for your help, they aren't getting their other work done. And you haven't done your job well, or they wouldn't need to bother you so often.

This section explains how to organize a file system that's convenient for users while being both secure and convenient to manage. Organizing users, and groups of users for particular purposes, will make your life easier when done efficiently. We also cover NetWare Directory Services and the security advantages provided by a global, single login user control system in this part.

Setting up the file system

A file system is the way the network operating system handles and stores files. NetWare fools your PC's operating system into thinking that the NetWare server hard drives are really local hard drives. Well, that's what goes on under the covers of Windows 95 and 98, although Microsoft pretends they have incorporated network file system support for NetWare and many others into their basic operating system. The effect is the same: Users see remote, server-based hard disks within their own desktop applications, management utilities like Explorer, and in their Network Neighborhood icons in Windows 95/98/NT.

A single NetWare server disk may be carved up into multiple NetWare volumes, although we don't recommend that for NetWare 4.*x* and NetWare 5. Whereas multiple volumes used to be handy for organizing application programs and user data, there are better ways to handle these problems with NetWare today (through NDS and grouping your network users based on job functions). Often, multiple NetWare server disks are combined into a single, seamless NetWare volume.

Server directories are created and organized much like file systems on any desktop computer. Directories may contain other directories and/or files, but files may not contain directories. The Windows interface makes all the directories look like Macintosh folders, but they're still directories, regardless of the icon.

NetWare's default file server directories are LOGIN, PUBLIC, MAIL, SYSTEM, and ETC. NetWare 5 adds JAVA and NETBASIC directories to contain files necessary for many of the new features for NetWare 5. The default directories are:

+ **LOGIN:** Stores user login support files.

+ **PUBLIC:** Stores utilities for all users.

+ **MAIL:** A holdover from when NetWare included an e-mail program; however, many messaging programs still use this directory.

+ **SYSTEM:** Contains critical system files for starting, running, and managing the file server itself; access is normally restricted to the network administrator.

+ **ETC:** Contains TCP/IP protocol files and support utilities.

+ **NETBASIC:** Offers scripts and support files for Novell's Visual Basic-compatible language starting with NetWare 4.11.

+ **JAVA (NetWare 5):** Includes Java utilities, including those for the new graphical installation utility, files for running a JVM (Java Virtual Machine) on the NetWare server, and support files for Java programmers.

Two statements of advice:

+ Keep your applications separate from the resulting data whenever possible.

Use clever directory organization to load as many applications as possible into a directory hierarchical tree different than the one you use for user data. In other words, don't blindly accept a Windows application request to load into \PROGRAM FILES unless you have such a directory running on your server. Then store data files, if created on a server directory for a group of users such as a shared database file, in a directory tree called \DATA. Why? Easier security (as you'll see) and it's quicker and easier to back up and restore data.

✦ Let your users feel that they have some level of ownership on the server.

Giving users some "personal" real estate on the server disk encourages them to store data there, rather than on their own hard drives. Users never back up their hard drives, and if the only copy of the Brunsweiger Report is on Alex Johnson's hard drive and that drive crashes, it is gone for good. More likely, however, Alex will accidentally delete the file. That file is still, you guessed it, gone for good.

If Alex deletes a file on the server, you may be able to salvage that file with a NetWare utility. Better yet, you can make sure Alex can only delete files he should be able to delete, and no more. But if Alex still deletes that file, your backup from the previous night will save his accident-prone skin.

So,

```
SYS:PROGRAM_FILES\MSOFFICE\WORD
```

is a good place to keep the shared version of Microsoft Word on the server. These application files can be controlled so users may only read the files, not modify or delete them. Different application files have different rules about this, however, so check your application documentation.

For example,

```
SYS:USERS\ALEXJ\DOCS
```

is a good place for Alex to keep the files he creates with Microsoft Word or any other word processor. He may also have directories for spreadsheets, presentations, or any other type of directory structure he wishes. The point is, that from the SYS:\USERS\ALEXJ directory on down, the server disk appears like a private hard disk for Alex, and he may do with it what he wishes.

Alex's files and directories are separate from

```
SYS:USERS\LAURAN\DOCS
```

Both users can save their own files away from other users and still be protected by a regular NetWare system backup. You'll notice that there is an N after Laura's name and a J after Alex's name. We do this because in large networks it is typical for more than one employee to have the same first name. Adding the initial of the last name after the first name can prevent confusion in large networks.

Now that corporate teams and GroupWare are big buzzwords, you should probably make some shared directories for user convenience. For example:

SYS:SHARED

This allows everyone on the network to put or get files from this directory. Control options include making shared directories for all departments:

✦ SYS:SHARED\MKTNG lets everyone in the Marketing group access the files in this directory.

✦ SYS:SHARED\REAL-WORK allows access to those assigned to the Real Work group.

Carefully read information with each application you will store on the file server. There can sometimes be problems reconciling your directory arrangement and the software's "default" file destination. You will suffer less if you let critical applications install the way the programmers demand, and adjust your system to take them into account.

Networked applications normally charge by the number of network users executing the program at the same time (concurrent users), so your network will need an application to track the programs in use at all times. Some programs lock out users beyond the purchased concurrent license count, whereas others don't. You, and your management, are responsible for buying the correct number of applications for your users, so get a metering package to monitor even the software that provides its own metering. Cheating will get you caught when a disgruntled employee starts trying to "get back" at the company. Stay legal, and sleep better.

Adding users and groups

The one preconfigured user on a new NetWare server is ADMIN, short for administrator. You, as the ADMIN, must add users to the network through one of the NetWare utilities.

You create individual users using one of the NetWare Administrator programs (NWADMIN, NWADMN32, NWADMN3X, NWADMN95, or NWADMNNT). Each program is about the same, depending on the client operating system you have on your management station.

NETADMIN, the old DOS version and replacement for SYSCON in NetWare 3.*x*, leaves out some important details when working with NetWare 5 (and 4.*x*, if you want the truth); therefore, don't use it for serious administration work. The typical method used to add users to the system goes something like this:

1. Open the appropriate version of the NetWare Administrator.

2. Click the context (container name) where you want to create the user.

3. Click Object menu, and then click Create.

4. Provide a login name and user last name (minimum requirements) in the Create User box that appears. You may also let NetWare create a home directory for that user by checking the box to do so, and check the boxes to define additional properties or create another user. Click HELP for an explanation of "legal" login names.

5. Click the Create button.

Extra information fields in the User Identification dialog include full name, phone numbers, description, and location. In a small network, these fields aren't used for much, but in large networks they make searching for specific users easier.

Creating groups is similar to creating individual users, but there is no login name for a group of users:

1. Right-click the context (container name) for the group, then click Create in the pop-up menu, and then name the group.

2. The trick now is providing members for the group. After clicking Create to make the group official, highlight the group and press Enter, or right-click on the group and choose Details.

3. Highlight the group name and press Enter, or right-click on the group and choose Details.

4. Click the Members button, and a blank screen appears.

5. Click Add, and the Select Object dialog appears, listing the Browse context in the right window and the Available objects in the left window.

6. Control-click (which allows you to select multiple users) the users to add to the group, and then click OK. Each tagged user appears in the Group members screen. Click OK to save the list of group users.

Rather than create a group and add users to that group, you can create a user and grant group rights to that user.

Group members have almost the same exact attributes as users for access to files and directories. Most of what we cover in the "NetWare security basics" section (in this part), such as security and access restrictions, applies to groups as well as to users.

Producing users in bulk, such as when converting a full list of users from another network into NetWare, requires a predetermined template to use as a guideline for each new user. NetWare 4.*x* and 5 use the UIMPORT utility, whereas NetWare 3.*x* offers both USERDEF and MAKEUSER utilities. All offer scripting control for applying user attributes in bulk during the import procedure. (See Part IV for more information about UIMPORT and MAKEUSER.)

Preparing for NetWare Directory Services

During installation, the Simple option creates a single NDS space with one container for the server, print support objects, and users. This configuration is like the earlier NetWare 3.*x* network arrangement, but has the added advantage of allowing all users access to all servers through one administration tool. Even if NDS did nothing more than allow users access to all servers with one administration tool, it would still be valuable.

However, many more features, most of them designed to make your life easier, come with NDS. With great power comes great responsibility for planning, so let's look at your network building blocks, called containers in NetWare-speak:

✦ **Country:** The geographical country, used only when networks are huge and multinational.

✦ **Organization:** Company, division, department, or your entire network. Organizations can include Organizational Units or Leaf objects (users, groups, and so on) and may be contained by [Root] or Country objects. This is your best organizing tool; many companies consider each Organization almost a separate network that connects to the others in the company only occasionally.

✦ **Organizational Unit:** Second level of container for object control. If your Organization is your entire company, Organizational Units may be departments. If your Organization is a department, the Organizational Units should be work teams.

Containers are the "holders" of network "things" and your network things are leaf objects, which represent real items (listed in order of importance), such as:

✦ Applications

✦ Group

✦ NetWare Server

✦ Printer, Print Queue, or Print Server

✦ User

✦ Volume (server disk volume)

There are other leaf objects, but these are the ones you use the most. Leaf objects may be created within Organizations or Organizational Units.

Get high level involvement in deciding your NDS layout. Popular options include getting a current organizational chart for your company, and starting your NDS design from there. Take geography into account, because you want some servers in each physical location to provide local access to network information. Draw your plan, and then get upper management feedback before starting. You're better off following existing company organization than you are creating a new network organization, and the existing company structure is already approved.

Tools and utilities for NDS control are covered in Parts III and VI.

NetWare security basics

Network security is high on your management's consciousness today, because all the nontechnical media from *The Wall Street Journal* to your local TV stations believe the Internet is full of hackers, thieves, and data pirates. How does this impact your NetWare network? Management is paranoid, and they become hyper-paranoid when you connect NetWare to the Internet.

Put a good security foundation in place from the beginning, and your life will be much less stressful. It's easier to loosen security restrictions over time than to tighten them, so start tough.

You'll notice that many attributes cover security situations — from accessing files to controlling the ability to even log in to the network. Each leaf object has a variety of attributes, including these used most often:

✦ Login name

✦ E-mail address

✦ Group membership

✦ Print Job Configuration

✦ Password restrictions

✦ Rights to Files and Directories

✦ Login restrictions

Rights in NetWare are inherited, meaning they flow downhill in almost all cases. If a user has rights to one directory, he or she has rights to all subdirectories and files therein. When a right is granted to an Organization, that right is passed to all Organizational Units inside the Organization. Rights the user possesses are called trustee rights.

Access rights to files and directories are the most common security control applied to users. You want the users to be able to handle all their own files, but not have access to other people's files.

The options for file and directory access rights are:

♦ **Supervisor (S):** All rights to file or directory

♦ **Read (R):** Open, read, or execute (copy or modify) the file

♦ **Write (W):** Open and write to the file

♦ **Create (C):** Create a file and salvage a file that's been deleted

♦ **Erase (E):** Delete a file

♦ **Modify (M):** Change attributes and rename file (this doesn't give access to file contents)

♦ **File Scan (F):** Allows the user to see the file when viewing the directory

♦ **Access Control (A):** Second to Supervisor right, allows user to control all other users' rights to a file or directory

There are slight differences in some controls for directories, but they all have to do with the IRF (Inherited Rights Filter) — sometimes called the Inherited Rights Mask (but is exactly the same thing), depending on which NetWare version you have.

Use the IRF to reduce rights for people within a subdirectory structure, such as when the \ACCOUNTING directory includes \AR, \AP, \GL, and \PAYROLL. Everyone in the accounting department has rights to everything in the \ACCOUNTING directory, meaning they inherit the same rights for all subdirectories.

Allowing free access to the \ACCOUNTING\PAYROLL directory may be more open than management wants. In this case, the IRF is applied, using the RIGHTS command to block all rights to the sensitive directory. The network administrator must then specifically grant rights for the \ACCOUNTING\PAYROLL directory for those users with clearance. Another security step you can use is to assign attributes to files.

You can use file attributes as quasi-security measures. The most common of these attributes are:

✦ **Normal (N):** Shorthand for Read and Write (RW), and the default setting for all files

✦ **Read Write (RW):** Longhand for Normal (N), and still the default setting

✦ **Read Only (RO):** Read but not modify. Handy for COM and EXE files to keep them from being deleted accidentally

✦ **Shareable (S):** Allows multiple users to open and modify files; best used under the control of the application that sets the attribute during installation

Read about the other file attributes in the documentation. If you have a NetWare 4.*x* or NetWare 5 network and have compression turned on to increase your usable disk space, you may want to check out the Immediate Compress (IC) and Don't Compress (DC) attributes in the Online Documentation CD-ROM.

NetWare completely embraces TCP/IP

It will take some time before all the NetWare users understand the implications of this statement, but NetWare has embraced TCP/IP in a huge way. In fact, although Microsoft 95/98/NT has several years' head start, the NetWare integration of TCP/IP into all parts of the client-server communication streams zooms ahead of the mediocre TCP/IP support Microsoft currently provides.

Why is this emotional embrace so important? Well, TCP/IP is the most widely used protocol in the world. It is the communication foundation of the Internet and the World Wide Web.

How complete is NetWare's embrace of TCP/IP? The default for NetWare 5 is for TCP/IP to provide a NetWare client to NetWare server communications. IPX, the most popular LAN protocol and supporter of many thousands of applications, is completely emulated on TCP/IP so that those applications work. But this isn't a TCP/IP "wrapper" around IPX, like NetWare/IP was. NetWare 5 has rewritten the NCP (NetWare Core Protocol) to use TCP/IP rather than IPX. This new transport technology is now the default choice for all NetWare 5 networks, indicating a high degree of trust in TCP/IP performance and security.

BorderManager takes many of the TCP/IP tools and utilities and makes them separate products, rather than rolling everything into NetWare 4.11, IntranetWare, or NetWare 5. Why do this? Because the features of BorderManager provide support for an entire network, not for the users of a single NetWare server. For more information about BorderManager, see Part I.

Does NetWare "do" TCP/IP now? Absolutely. In fact, NetWare does TCP/IP better than any Microsoft product, and just as well as most Unix servers.

Part III

The Major NetWare Utilities and Tools

Every complex system has a set of tools, ranging from small toolkits for computers to huge wrenches for oil derricks. NetWare is no exception, but at least you won't get all greasy maintaining your network.

Most of these tools and utilities are aimed at you, the administrator; but we also list several user utilities as well. Windows 95/98/NT are starting to take over for earlier NetWare utilities, such as CAPTURE, because these systems now do a better job of viewing and managing network resources.

Novell has done well in controlling and managing printers for years, which is good for those users who don't believe computer information is real until it appears on paper. These users will be glad to know that Novell has added new printer controls to NetWare 5.

In this part . . .

- ✔ NetWare Internet features
- ✔ NetWare Directory Services function and design
- ✔ NetWare print utilities
- ✔ NetWare user utilities

Internet-Friendly Features and Functions

The progression from NetWare 4.0 to NetWare 5 reflects the changes from an Internet-unaware to a full Internet-friendly network operating system. Although NetWare 5 can't be called an "Internet" operating system directly, the combination of NetWare 4.11, IntranetWare, or NetWare 5 along with the security and performance tools provided in BorderManager make an outstanding link between local clients, the Internet, and all points in between.

Many of the advantages Novell brings to NetWare through high-performance file access and a solid security structure apply directly to Internet use. A Web server provides files, on request, from intelligent clients across a network; NetWare does exactly the same thing. Novell has nearly two decades of experience making that network connection faster and more reliable.

As with NetWare, a Web *server* is almost always a software process. Many NetWare features are really servers, but only a few are labeled as such. Print server is one good example of a process that is software only, but still is called a server. The same goes for Web servers — many are supported by a single hardware server, most often running some version of Unix.

Web Server 2.5 for NetWare 4.11/IntranetWare

The best news about the two Web server options for NetWare servers is that both are free. These options don't include an ever-growing number of third-party Web servers supported by NetWare. Watch for a full Java Web server option sometime soon that will run perfectly well under the JVM (Java Virtual Machine) in NetWare 5, showing again what a strong platform a NetWare server can be.

Technically, a Web server is one that relies on the HTTP (HyperText Transfer Protocol). Developed in 1992 and 1993, HTTP relies on the TCP/IP protocol suite for transmission control and connection. The protocol is "stateless," meaning that each new request to an HTTP server must reestablish transmission details for packet exchange. This is why some HTTP transfers take so long, but the lack of a "hard" connection between the HTTP servers and the HTTP client (Web browser) means better security and fewer problems when the connection is dropped during transmission.

The NetWare Web Server 2.5 includes full support for:

✦ BASIC and PERL scripts

✦ Java applications

✦ R-CGI (Remote Common Gateway Interface): a link to external programs on other Web servers

✦ L-CGI (Local Common Gateway Interface): a program link to processes running as NLMs (NetWare Loadable Modules) on the local file server

Follow these steps to install the Novell Web Server 2.5 on your NetWare server:

1. Verify TCP/IP support is active and configured properly on the Web server-to-be by communicating with the server using TCP/IP rather than IPX/SPX from another network device.

2. Type **LOAD INSTALL** at the server colon prompt.

3. Choose Product Options — Choose an Item or Product Listed Above, and press Enter.

4. Choose Install NetWare Web Server 2.5 and press Enter.

5. Provide the source of your NetWare Web Server files, which is your primary NetWare CD.

6. Provide a Web Server administrator password.

7. Reboot your server and watch the Web Server load and start automatically.

Novell includes a new utility, WEBMGR.EXE, to manage the Web Server. This file is loaded to the \PUBLIC directory during Web Server installation. You may want to move WEBMGR.EXE, or limit access to supervisors only, to stop users from accidentally playing with your Web server configuration.

Here's how you use the Web Manager utility program (if you're an ADMIN user or equivalent, of course):

1. Log in as the ADMIN user or equivalent.

2. Run the WEBMGR.EXE application from the /PUBLIC directory.

> The WEBMGR.EXE application wants to know three things about the directory structure for your Web server: where to put HTML documents, where to put log files, and where to allow users to make their own HTML Web pages available. The last part is optional, because you can turn off user access to Web server pages.

3. Click the Open icon, and give the location for the configuration files for the Web Server to be managed.

4. Click each page tab and modify settings as necessary.

- **Server:** This tab is used to configure the IP address of the server, the TCP port used (80 is the default), and the administrator's e-mail address for feedback. Another nice feature on the Server tab is the capability to use a Web browser to peruse the NDS tree and information. A check box labeled Enable NDS browsing lets any Web client see the NDS structure of your network.

- **Directories:** This tab sets the locations for all the scripts, images, and indices used by the Web Server software. Personal user Web pages will be created, and this screen directs the storage locations of user pages.

- **User Access:** NDS doesn't control access to the Web Server 2.5, so a third tab offers User Access. The Web Manager program reads the available user list from NetWare Directory Services (NDS), however, and provides that list in the Network users list box. One check box, All valid users, makes short work of granting Web access to everyone. In a departmental Web Server, groups and users may be blocked out as you deem necessary.

- **System Access:** This tab details who has access to the system configuration.

- **Logs:** This last tab is full of mundane log file questions. Decisions about the length of log files, and whether the log file should wrap and overwrite, or send an error message, are made here along with other burning, but boring, log file questions.

If you have a NetWare 4.1*x* server and would like a copy of Web Server, feel free to download it from the Novell Web Server at www.novell.com. Any TCP/IP-enabled NetWare 4.0 and above server can run this software without a purchase fee or extra user pricing.

FastTrack

NetWare 5 includes the Netscape FastTrack Web Server. Novell made a deal with Netscape, for a joint code-swap and technology partnership. The two formed Novonyx, an independent company, to handle certain development issues and hold the code license as a third party.

The result of the partnership is a free copy of the Netscape FastTrack Web Server with each copy of NetWare 5. Integration with NDS and the NetWare server operating system is tighter than with the earlier Web Server 2.5 software. Yes, the Novonyx

Netscape server software is also available for current NetWare 4.*x* server customers. It can be downloaded for free from the Novell Web site.

Features of FastTrack Server include:

+ Complete content management tools

+ Encryption supported through SSL (Secure Sockets Layer) 3.0 protocol

+ Java support, including support for JavaScript, Java servlets, and JavaBeans for developing more enterprise Java applications

+ Link management software tools and utilities for link verification

+ Scripting language support for all popular Web server languages

The best third-party support in the Web server market, NetWare 5 includes the Netscape FastTrack Web server software on a separate CD-ROM disk in the installation pack — rather than putting the program in the "Other Installation Items/Products" section like the Novell Web Server 2.5 does.

Server requirements for FastTrack include:

+ 100MB free disk space on the SYS volume

+ 64MB minimum RAM

+ NetWare Service Pack 4 (when installing on a NetWare 4.1*x* server)

Once you have a NetWare client workstation with plenty of RAM, free disk space, CD-ROM drive, and an active connection to your target server, the installation process is pretty simple for FastTrack:

1. Run the \PRODUCTS\NOVONYX\SETUP application from the CD-ROM drive on your workstation.

A huge file moves from your CD to your hard disk, under control of an installation wizard program.

2. Supply the FastTrack administrator name and password.

3. Provide a new port number for use only by the FastTrack administrator in place of the default port number 80.

The unusual port number is a management security trick, not completely secure, but a good deterrent when used with a good administrator name and password.

4. Specify if you want the FastTrack Web Server to start automatically when the server starts.

When administering a FastTrack Web Server with any Web browser, the administrator must log in to a specific Web URL (Uniform Resource Locator) and port number: for example, www.lanw.com:9952. (Don't try this, because the whole idea is that the port number is known only to the Web administrator.)

You can find no shortage of books to help you configure and program your new Netscape FastTrack server, including *HTML For Dummies,* 3rd Edition, by Ed Tittel and Steve James (IDG Books Worldwide, Inc.), and *Creating Cool Web Pages with HTML,* by Dave Taylor (IDG Books Worldwide, Inc.).

Routing services

Part of the advantage of NetWare as a Web server platform is its capability to route lots of traffic, both local and remote packets, through any file server. IntranetWare and NetWare 5 both include the capability to work as a router for IPX, TCP/IP, AppleTalk, PPP (Point to Point Protocol), ATM (Asynchronous Transfer Mode), Frame Relay, X.25 (an older packet-switch data network protocol), and even wireless network connections.

You use the following utilities (depending on your NetWare version) to configure and manage the routing software in your NetWare server:

✦ **NIASCFG (NetWare Internet Access Server ConFiGuration):** Controls WAN (Wide Area Network) board and protocol connections, including binding network protocols to an interface.

✦ **FILTCFG (FILTer ConFiGuration):** Controls the setup and configuration of packet filters for IPX, TCP/IP, and AppleTalk protocols. Filters may block packets from coming in or from leaving the network.

✦ **STATICON (Static Routing Configuration):** Controls IPX static routes and the services at each end of the connection.

✦ **CALLMGR (Call Manager):** Monitors WAN connections and initiates or terminates WAN calls manually.

✦ **CPECFG (Customer Premise Equipment ConFiGuration):** Configures and manages communications equipment from the server console, such as modems and stand-alone routers.

Four other monitoring utilities focus on individual protocols:

+ **PPPCON:** Point to Point Protocol links

+ **IPXCON:** IPX routers, bridges, and static routes

+ **ATCON:** AppleTalk protocol monitor

+ **TCPCON:** TCP/IP monitor

Each item in this list is discussed in some detail in the Novell Internet Access Server Troubleshooting and Management and Optimization manual sections.

Application access

Many customers told Novell that network applications should be easier for nontechnical users to find and launch, and at the same time, those applications should be more manageable and easier to control than applications running strictly on a client workstation.

Novell took care of these requests with NAL (NetWare Application Launcher). NAL incorporates more control for administrators with easier access for users. How's that for a double play?

The two steps in the application process are: configuring the application object with NDS (a new feature in NetWare 4.11), and making those objects available to the proper users under the proper circumstances.

You create application objects using NetWare Application Manager, which is really just one of the functions within NetWare Administrator. Follow these steps to create an application object:

1. Open NetWare Administrator.

2. Choose the container to contain the Application object.

3. Press Insert or click the right mouse button to pop open the menu, and then click Create.

4. Choose the correct Application tag icon: DOS, Windows 3.*x*, 95, or NT.

5. Provide an Application object icon title.

6. Type the path using UNC (Universal Naming Convention), such as **\SERVER1\SYS\COREL\OFFICE8\WPWIN8\ WPWIN.EXE,** or use the Browse button and dialog to find the executable file.

7. Set drive mappings, print settings, or scripts to run before and/or after the application executes. Click the Drives/Ports or Scripts button to add these instructions.

8. Set the associations for users able to see and use the Application Launcher by clicking the Associations button, and then adding (with the Add button) the objects (users and groups) that can use this application.

9. Save the Application object.

Because many applications today have icon files included, you should have no problem finding a recognizable image to represent the application. If not, there is a Change Icon button on the Identification page to help you pick another icon. You also have a chance to place descriptions and the contact name for a support person (Description and Contacts buttons) for that particular application — all of which will be available to your user.

The second part of the equation is to make the Application Launcher available to your users. Surprise; you already have. Once you tag the users and groups *Associated* with the Application Launcher, users will find the Application Launcher in their NAL folder in Windows 95/98/NT or the NAL Group in Windows 3.1.

Users can view, but not change, all the settings for the Application Launcher objects. To view these settings, the user right-clicks the Application Launcher object and clicks the Properties menu item.

NetWare Directory Design Principles

NDS sees only three types of objects:

+ **Root:** Defines the name of the Directory database

+ **Container:** Organizes parts of the database in a series of containers (similar in function to directories and subdirectories holding files)

+ **Leaf:** Represents users printers, servers, applications, and so on

So, why is this all called a Directory tree? Because there is a root, there are containers that act like branches, and there are leaf objects — where all the fun happens. This is a common model for object-oriented hierarchical database structures.

Reading your rights

Every object in the Directory tree has a set of access rights that determines who may make changes to an object. Object rights describe what the object is allowed to do. The object rights are:

+ **Supervisor:** All rights to the object and its properties

✦ **Create:** The right to create new objects within a specified container

✦ **Delete:** The right to delete objects within a specified container

✦ **Rename:** The right to change the object's assigned name, which changes the references to that object in the Directory tree

Separate from the rights to control an object within a container are the rights to the object properties. These Property Rights affect access and control of the properties of an object, not the object itself. Property Rights are:

✦ **Add/Delete self:** Lets a user add his or her name as a value for a property, but no other value changes are allowed.

✦ **Compare:** Compares a supplied value to an actual property value, and obtains a True or False response, but not the actual value.

✦ **Read:** Allows the user to read the property values.

✦ **Supervisor:** Grants the user all rights to the property.

✦ **Write:** Allows the user to add, change, or remove property values.

Naming your tree

First thing you do is name your Directory tree, which you do during installation. The rules for tree names are:

✦ Must be unique for all connected networks

✦ May use letters A–Z

✦ May use numbers 0–9

✦ May use hyphens and underscores

✦ May be any length, but the complete context name must be less than 255 characters

Do yourself a favor, and stay away from long, involved tree names with hyphens, underscores, or numbers. This is not a password, so don't make it hard to guess. This name will be seen and used regularly, so make it mean something to your users. They won't see it often, but it should make sense to them when they do see it.

Making time count

When you install NDS for the first time on a server, you should know several things, such as:

✦ The name for your NDS tree

✦ Your time zone

✦ Your company (Organization) name

✦ Optionally, all Organizational Unit names (divisions, departments, and so on)

✦ The Organization or Organizational Unit you wish to hold the server

✦ The password for the Admin user for NDS, or supply one if you are creating NDS with this server installation

Why the time zone? Timestamps are critical components of NDS, because accurate timestamps are the only way for the database to tell which events happened in which order. Only when the timestamps for transactions are trustworthy can the Directory work properly. This is especially critical for networks spanning long distances; WAN problems can cause NDS problems, or at least delay many NDS transactions while timestamps are sorted out.

NetWare offers a list of time zones covering the entire world. Daylight Savings Time is enabled by default, but you can turn it off if your location does not spring forward and fall back.

Creating design goals

Here are four goals for your NDS design:

✦ Build in fault-tolerance for the Directory database.

✦ Keep traffic across WAN links to a minimum.

✦ Keep information close to the users.

✦ Make your network easy to maintain.

Don't feel bad if your first NDS tree doesn't meet all four of these goals, or even two of these goals. No first-time Directory gets everything necessary in exactly the right place. Everything in NDS can be changed, although some changes are messier than others.

Planning has two phases: the logical phase and the physical phase. The logical phase steps are:

1. Determine the best NDS structure for your network.

2. Identify the naming conventions for your network.

3. Plan your implementation method.

NetWare Directory Design Principles

All these phases are dependent upon answers from other people, such as your manager or the executive management team trying to reorganize your company yet again. This part can take forever if you don't put a deadline on the project.

The physical phase is user-driven, because here you want to make sure the Directory supports the needs of your users. The three important steps are:

1. Determine your security situation (all too often easier said than done).

2. Set up your Directory replication map.

3. Synchronize Directory time.

Unfortunately, some of these last six steps are intertwined; one depends on another, which depends on another. How can you define security if you don't know the NDS structure, which you don't know because you haven't gotten the organization chart you requested?

Identifying the naming conventions for your network may require some time and arguments, but it is important. The person coming after you will bless your memory if names for users and network resources are well-planned, self-explanatory, and consistent. A consistent naming structure will save you many hours of frustration.

Organizing by location

The organizing by location method is sometimes called the bottom-up or departmental method, but what you call it is less important than the advantages this method provides some companies. This method may work for your organization if your company

✦ Is geographically dispersed with self-contained groups or

✦ Has a strong departmental slant, with each department fairly self-contained

In these cases, make sure each group or department has its own Organization container, if not its own separate Directory tree. Starting with the Client32 software in NetWare 4.11 and IntranetWare, users can finally see more than one tree at a time, which means they can use resources from different departments.

If you don't want your users climbing all over your tree (a painful thought if they get stuck up there), you should make use of the Alias objects. Representing resources from another tree with an Alias is easier than teaching your users about multitree network design. Check the online NDS documentation for Alias details.

Organizing by function

This method is also called the top-down method. This system works well when you have:

+ A strong central MIS or planning group

+ Local connections, or fast and reliable WAN links

+ Employees from all departments mixed together in the office

This method of NDS organization handles the trend of putting support personnel in the middle of other job functions. If your company has an engineer sitting beside a marketing person sitting beside an accounts payable person, a functional organization may be best. (Not to mention the need for a better space design, so natural enemies like engineers and marketers aren't in close proximity.)

Controlling context

Context refers to the location of objects within the Directory tree. Because every object is in a container, the details about which container holds the object is the context.

Using the CX command (a lot like the DOS directory command CD) a user can move up and down through his or her NDS tree. The CX command allows you to view and set your current context.

Typing **CX** by itself on a DOS command line displays the current context, just as typing **CD** on a command line displays the current directory. Typing **CX .** moves you up a level, even though you would expect the command to be **CX ..** like it is for the CD command.

To move to another context, type **CX** with the context name including all identifiers (**CX ou=dummy.o=lanw**, for example). Type **CX /?** on the command line for help.

Organizing your network into Organizations and Organizational Units means you'll have some context issues to deal with. The advantage to this method, and the value of contexts, is that you can assign values and property rights to an entire context, which gives all objects within that context the same powers. This is similar to giving a group of users a feature once rather than spending the time giving every single user the same feature repeatedly.

Users will get lost in contexts if you don't help them. Make sure the login configuration, whether in a NET.CFG file for the obsolete VLM client software, or the new tabbed fields for Client32, is correct. If the login configuration is wrong, users will come crying to you and ask why you "broke" their network.

If you have users with really obsolete clients, and are thereby forced to stick with the Bindery database, context is still important. If you re-create a typical NetWare 3.x network within a single Organization, you can then assign a Bindery context to that container. Everyone using Bindery authentication can then see all network resources within that Organization.

Creating partitions and replicas

A *partition* is a distinct unit of data in the NDS tree. It must include at least one container object, all objects inside that container, and the data about all those objects. No file information is included within a partition, and an object can be in only one partition.

A *replica* is a copy of one partition. Keeping replicas close to groups of users makes response times faster when logging in and searching for network resources. Making copies of partitions with replicas also provides NDS outstanding fault tolerance, because all critical information is copied around the network.

The four types of replicas are:

+ **Master replica:** Primary replica for a given partition. Only one replica can be the Master.

+ **Read/Write replica:** Reads and writes Directory transactions, such as object adds and deletes, and sends that information to the Master replica. If the Master replica is lost, a Read/Write replica must become the Master.

+ **Read Only replica:** A backup replica that helps users by keeping information close to them, but doesn't make Directory changes.

+ **Subordinate Reference replica:** Special backup replica placed by NDS automatically. You don't need to worry about this one.

Partitions, because they work along container lines, are most helpful when containers are grouped by geography. Keeping partitions and assorted replicas close to groups of users increases network performance for your users without causing any security or management problems whatsoever. The traffic between the remote partitions and the home office will be far less than the traffic generated by users forced to check remote servers for every Directory operation.

Here are some partition and replica management guidelines:

+ Replicate the partition holding the [Root] object several times. If something happens to this partition, your NDS tree withers quickly and dies.

✦ Make at least three replicas of every partition. Try to keep one replica in a different physical location if your network has that option.

✦ Create partitions following the natural boundaries of your user population.

✦ Servers running Bindery Services must have a Master or Read/Write replica of the partition.

✦ Each object in the replica takes about 1K of disk space. Only changes go across the network between partitions and replicas, but creating or rebuilding a replica makes for lots of traffic. Schedule these operations carefully to avoid aggravating more users than necessary.

How to create, merge, and manage partitions and replicas is covered in Part IV.

NetWare Directory Services

Officially, NDS is a distributed and replicated security database. It is *distributed* because each NetWare 4.*x* and above server runs NDS, and it is *replicated* because partitions of the database can be copied to different servers. These safeguards, and the strength of NDS, mean that you will probably never see an NDS failure that takes down all or part of your network.

NDS is object-oriented (hence all the user objects, printer objects, application objects, and so on). Each object can be seen and accessed by every other object, if the second object has the proper authority. Normally, the first object is a directory, printer, or application, and the second object is a user. Technically any object can use the resources of any other object. You'll go around in circles if you think about that the wrong way, so don't worry about it too much.

NDS overview

If you're new to NDS, here are some NDS hot buttons:

✦ **Advanced security:** One login name and password gives users full access to the entire network, yet maintains state-of-the-art security through hierarchical control lists.

✦ **Compatibility:** NetWare 4.*x* and NetWare 5 NDS servers can incorporate servers running NetWare 3.*x* and even NetWare 2.*x* into the network through Bindery Services, emulating the older Bindery database for communications with earlier systems.

✦ **Delegation:** Subadministrators may have complete control over specified portions of the network, easily spreading the workload among administrators while maintaining system security.

✦ **Flexibility:** Changes to the NDS database can be made quickly and easily, and portions of the network can be split or moved simply.

✦ **Open-ended:** The NDS schema, or set of rules about the data, can be extended by applications, adding new functionality.

✦ **Reliability:** The NDS database is replicated automatically and distributed. Losing the Directory information from one or several servers does not disturb NDS.

✦ **Scalability:** NDS can model a simple, flat network structure for small companies, and scale up to hundreds of thousands of objects on a network spanning many countries.

✦ **Simple administration:** All resources maintain a single identity through the network, and all supervisors use the same management utility to view the network.

✦ **Usability:** The NDS database structure, hidden from the users and administrators, makes searching and retrieving object attributes fast and efficient. Search tools are provided, including wildcards.

NWADMIN

The primary network administration tools for NetWare 3.*x* are SYSCON and PCONSOLE. NetWare in the Directory era uses NetWare Administrator, known here as NWADMIN.

You find several versions of NWADMIN on your file server, no matter which version of NetWare 4.*x* or NetWare 5 you have. The different versions are as follows:

✦ NWADMIN

✦ NWADMN32

✦ NWADMN3X

✦ NWADMN95

✦ NWADMNNT

NWADMIN was the first iteration for Windows 3.1, followed by NWADMN3X. NWADMN32 works with the NetWare Client32 software. You can tell which versions work with Windows 95 and NT by the final two characters in each filename.

The more general NWADMN32 is in your server's \PUBLIC directory. Search \PUBLIC\WIN95 and \PUBLIC\WINNT for the appropriate other versions. We call the administration tool NWADMIN, with the understanding that you know which tool to run on which management client platform.

Almost every object in NetWare can be created, modified, or deleted within NWADMIN. Novell really wants to make NWADMIN your one-stop shop for network administration, and they are doing a good job.

The most flexible part of NWADMIN is the capability for developers to add "snap-ins" to the program, usually through a new or modified DLL (Dynamic Link Library) file in the directory holding NWADMIN. After modification, new features generally appear in the Tools menu.

Here are a few tips to help you with NWADMIN:

✦ When you modify NWADMIN, modify only one copy, usually the one running only on your workstation. Don't assume a modification is available to everyone else running their own copy of NWADMIN, because that may not be true.

✦ Get a fast machine with lots of RAM, equal to the fastest PCs in the company to run NWADMIN. Using a high-speed connection for a server makes sense for this workstation, because so many network packets flow to and from this machine. Put your management machine on the server backbone, especially if it runs faster than the rest of your office network.

✦ Create an icon for NWADMIN on your management workstation, and link it to the proper executable file on the network. You may copy the executable file to your hard disk if you wish, but make sure you get all the DLL files from the directory as well.

While not eye-popping, the NWADMIN program is certainly graphical. Menu bars and icon bars cover the top of the application, and the white part of the screen is your Browser window. Not exactly like a Netscape browser window, NWADMIN can open multiple Browser windows, all spotlighting a different part of the same network.

When the utility opens, you probably see a view of the container your workstation inhabits at the start. Items are displayed in a typical hierarchical tree display, in this order:

✦ Groups

✦ Servers

✦ Printer

✦ Print server

✦ Print Queue

✦ Users

✦ Volumes

Each item is alphabetized within the groupings. You can create a new browser window on an Organization, Organizational Unit, or volume. To create a new browser window, highlight the object and press Insert or right-click to open the menu, and then choose Browse. If the Browse menu choice is grayed out, the object does not support a browse window.

NWADMIN has six menu options:

✦ **Object:** Shows configuration options for the highlighted object as well as the choices, such as Print, you expect to see on a File menu option.

✦ **View:** Controls the appearance of the browser window, plus provides some context navigation options, such as Set Context, Go Up a Level, and Sort and Include.

✦ **Options:** Settings for the NWADMIN handle its own configuration, as well as how trustees are displayed. (A trustee is a user or group object with access to a directory, file, or object.)

✦ **Tools:** Offers a variety of utilities, including Internet connections, starting a new browser window, salvage files, remote console, install licenses for software, and Print Services Quick Setup (if the highlight bar is on a container). New tools will be added to this list as more features are added to your network, so this menu list will change over time.

✦ **Window:** Arranges windows in a cascade or tile format, closes them all, opens a new one, and offers a pick list of open windows.

✦ **Help:** Provides help but also offers a direct link to the Novell Support Web page, switches on or off the welcome screen, and tells About NetWare Administrator.

The most used right-click menu choice option is the Details dialog window, which you can also open by highlighting an object and pressing Enter. If you used to work with the SYSCON program, you should feel right at home, because all the details are here. If you're new to NetWare, be assured that just about every configuration option for every object appears in the Details dialog window.

You spend most of your administration time in the Details dialog window. Every manageable detail about an object appears in the appropriate dialog window. For a user, for instance, common tasks are done through NWADMIN's Details menu options, a few of them are shown in the following list:

✦ **Login Script:** Used to be a critical feature for every user, but now, the container often has the login script, rather than the user. Login scripts arrange drive mappings and printer connections for users. Container login scripts pass the defined network arrangements to every user in the container as they log in.

✦ **Rights To Files And Directories:** The primary file security configuration screen.

✦ **Identification:** Used for username, login name, and other details.

✦ **Login Restrictions:** Used to lock out a user who left or set the expiration date for a password.

✦ **Password Restrictions:** Sets password restrictions. This option includes how many times a user can ignore the `change password now` message when the old password is expired.

✦ **Login Time Restrictions:** This option is used to restrict the times in which a user can log in to the network. This enables you to block everyone off the network during tape backup times, for instance.

✦ **Print Job Configuration:** Provides print job configuration details.

✦ **Group Membership:** You can do this also in the Group's detail window by clicking the Members button.

✦ **Applications:** Shows which programs will show up in the user's NetWare Application Launcher window.

More command buttons are available on each dialog window, but these are the major ones for users. More details are available in the online documentation.

NETADMIN

For the DOS-aholics out there, Novell still provides a DOS administration tool to replace SYSCON. NETADMIN tries to carry the load for SYSCON, but doesn't quite have the same feeling.

DOS-aholics, enjoy NETADMIN while you can, but realize that there are already jobs you can't perform with NETADMIN. The move is on to push you to NWADMIN.

The decades-old C-Worthy interface appears again as the foundation for NETADMIN, and remember the Escape key takes you back a menu level. If you've been pining for blue screens and yellow box borders, you should be happy now.

The first menu options you see in the NETADMIN options window when the program starts are:

✦ **Manage objects:** Most popular choice. This leads to a pick list of all objects in the container, which leads to the action menu items for each of those objects.

✦ **Manage according to search pattern:** Helps you set search parameters, such as the object class (server, user, and so on) you wish to find.

✦ **Change context:** Opens a new flat, horizontal window asking you to `Enter context:` and room to type. Press Insert to see a pick list of all contexts available.

✦ **Search:** Opens the way to find particular property attributes.

NETADMIN has no provisions for snap-ins, so the management tools you see are all the tools you can get. These tools are more for backward compatibility than everyday use.

DSMERGE

DSMERGE (Directory Services MERGE tree) offers a feature missing in the first release of NDS with NetWare 4.0: The capability to merge Directory trees. Truthfully, however, this procedure acts like most business mergers: One tree comes out dominant and essentially absorbs the other tree. The dominant tree is usually the one with the largest number of clients.

Go through both trees and make sure there are no similar names to cause confusion. You can have two users named LAURA for instance, but not if they are both in an Organizational Unit named ACCOUNTING. After the merge, two LAURA.ACCOUNTING users will cause a Directory problem. Rename one of the two objects or, better yet, rename one of the containers before the merge. Make a note for the future: Don't use just first names for user login names anymore.

DS Standard

DS Standard was the first offline NDS modeling tool that appeared outside Novell. In fact, Novell has yet to match this product with one of its own.

Developed and sold originally by Preferred Systems as DS Standard, the product is now DS Standard for NDS, part of the Cheyenne product line. Cheyenne, itself a division of Computer Associates, has gathered quite a few network management products.

The "offline" part is the best advantage of DS Standard. Working from a PC management station, DS Standard reads the current NDS database, and loads that into the management station in its own database structure. Once captured, the NDS database becomes a testing ground for new NDS structures, all modeled on the local computer. Experiment to your heart's content, yet never touch your official NDS database until you're ready to change.

Once your new database design is ready to implement, a few mouse clicks sends the DS Standard program to work, remaking your NDS structure to match the one modeled in NDS. One step, with full safeguards, and your new tree is in place.

DS Standard offers quite a few other advantages for managing NDS. If your network moves from small- to medium-sized, DS Standard is worth a look.

RexxWare Migration Toolkit

New with NetWare 5 is the RexxWare Migration Toolkit, based on SimWare's RexxWare migration product. This utility doesn't exactly model existing NDS databases into new configurations, but does help migrate NetWare 3.*x* Bindery-based networks to the new world of NetWare 5.

RexxWare takes your Bindery information and makes a comparable NDS tree. The tree is real, at least on the workstation, and all Bindery data items, such as users, printers, and groups, are converted into the appropriate NDS object.

When the model looks good, the NDS information is sent to your new or existing NDS tree. When you give approval, all the NetWare 3.*x* database information is vacuumed from the old server and deposited in the new tree. Quick, clean, easy, and another great inducement to upgrade.

Visio's Solution Pack for NDS

Starting in May 1998, Visio Corporation released a product developed with Novell's consulting group to take actual NDS design guidelines and rules and apply them to a Solution Pack to go along with Visio Professional 5.0. All the easy network design tools from Visio, such as drag-and-drop placement of network objects, can be applied to NDS.

Once again, the NDS information is copied to a workstation, modeled using the software (Visio in this case) and exported when all is well. The advantage Visio touts is the design rules for

NDS inside the program. Take your NDS structure, dump it into Visio, and let the rules and guidelines try to make a better network while you take a coffee break.

No automated tool is ready to replace network administrators, but an intelligent start to your network redesign should be welcome. Look for this product on Visio's Web site (www.visio.com), and see if it helps smooth your network transitions.

NetWare Print Utilities

One of the main features that helped sell NetWare in the 1980s was the availability of HP's LaserJet printers. The cost of LaserJets was so high at the beginning that companies found it cheaper to buy a network to share printers rather than buy printers for all who wanted one. Especially after you threw in the advantage of backing up data from the server on a network instead of letting it sit unprotected in stand-alone PCs.

Printing has been both a boon and a pain for networks ever since. You get more complaints from users about printing than anything else.

Luckily, NetWare has steadily improved the tools for managing network printing. In this section, not only do we look at the printing management tools Novell has had since NetWare 2.0, we also discuss the new Novell Distributed Print System.

NetWare Print Services overview

More flexibility with every version is a good summary of NetWare printing history. Early NetWare versions did well handling print jobs, but only when printers were tied directly to the server, which unfortunately slowed them down when big files constantly interrupted the processor to travel out the parallel or serial port to reach the printer.

Flexibility came by separating the components needed to handle printing. The file server hardware and print server software split, allowing print servers to run on workstation PCs, network-attached dedicated boxes, or the printers themselves. Management got more and more separated as well, and then converged back into the NWADMIN program.

Managing printer access and configurations with NWADMIN

Grizzled NetWare veterans may find it odd to have graphical printer control utilities, having been raised on PCONSOLE and the like, but here they are.

To manage any part of the print process, open NWADMIN and highlight the print object. Press Enter, or right-click and choose Details from the pop-up menu, to open a dialog box holding more than you need to know about the print object.

One of the common administrative jobs when managing printers is to check the job list for a printer, normally to delete a job or a user. To do this, follow these steps:

1. Open NWADMIN.

2. Highlight the appropriate print queue object and press Enter, or right-click the print queue object.

3. Click the Job List button on the right side of the dialog.

4. Highlight the job to be deleted (there is usually more than one by the time the user asks for help; check all jobs) and click the Delete button at the bottom of the dialog.

5. Close the dialog by clicking OK.

Every other print management process is available through NWADMIN, although we cover the DOS utilities in the next few paragraphs for old time's sake, and because print management is one area the DOS utilities still work as well as those within NWADMIN.

NDPS (Novell Distributed Print Service) separates components even more, by allowing users to address printers directly, rather than sending files to the print queue and then to the printer. Some users got confused by this process, and those users will certainly enjoy NDPS. Smarter and faster printers use NDPS to communicate with the print server, file server, and end user during the print process. All this communication can get confusing, but NDPS does a good job of keeping print jobs flowing and confusion to a minimum.

PCONSOLE

Two great advantages to the DOS printing management utilities are:

✦ Loading and running on any machine

✦ Loading much more quickly than NWADMIN (More speed in loading is always handy for management utilities.)

Because PCONSOLE.EXE resides in the \PUBLIC directory, you should be able to start the program anywhere you have a DOS command line interface. \PUBLIC should be in your search path — put there by the NetWare client installation software.

After you type **PCONSOLE**, you have these options in the Available Options box:

- ✦ Print Queues
- ✦ Printers
- ✦ Print Servers
- ✦ Quick Setup
- ✦ Change Context

Print Queues are the critical part of the chain, because NetWare (before NetWare Distributed Print Services, NDPS) addresses the Print Queue rather than the printer directly.

Part VI describes Quick Setup. The last menu option may be the most used, because using the Change Context option is something you'll probably have to do every time you address a different printer object.

Press Enter on Change Context, and the Enter Context window appears, waiting for you to type something. Don't type, press Insert instead, and pick your new context from the Object, Class pick list that appears.

Once you enter the proper context, each of the first three menu options works the same way: choose the option, see the list of printer objects of the type you requested, and then take action on the object of your choice.

Print Queues is first, and choosing Q1 in the second window pops open the Print Queue Information window. Here you find:

- ✦ **Print Jobs:** Current print jobs in the queue.

- ✦ **Status:** Details, such as number of print jobs, active print servers, and settable flags for queue configuration.

- ✦ **Attached Print Servers:** Shows the Print Servers currently servicing the print queue. Handy because more than one server can feed a queue.

- ✦ **Information:** Shows Object ID, which doesn't help much, but it also lists the name of the NetWare server and print queue volume, which are good to know.

- ✦ **Users:** Shows all the network users with access to the printer. Normally this shows groups or containers, rather than individual users. Adding individual users to print queues is not effective time management: Assign by groups or containers when at all possible.

✦ **Operators:** More than just the Admin user can handle print details, and this area is one of the best examples of distributed management available in NetWare 4.*x* and NetWare 5. Why run to a department to mess with a printer when you can assign the local power user to be Printer Boss, and grant that person the rights to control printing, but nothing else?

✦ **Print Servers:** Lists all the print servers feeding this print queue. Press Insert to add another print server to the list.

When you choose Printers from the front menu, a pick list of printers in your current context pops open. Choosing one of the printers opens a Printer ? Configuration window, with the ? replaced with the printer name.

There's no extra menu list for printer configuration; all the details are right in this menu. Anything you change becomes active almost immediately. One of the most helpful options is the last one, labeled Notification. Put your name in this list, and you'll get all sorts of NetWare messages about print failures. This is a helpful option, because you want to be sure you're not listed here, so you don't get bombarded with messages.

The Print Servers menu choice opens another pick list showing all the Print Servers in this context. Choosing a Print Server opens the Print Server Information menu, with these choices:

✦ **Printers:** Shows the printer services by this Print Server. You may choose a printer name to reach the Printer Configuration window.

✦ **Information and Status:** Describes the type of Print Server, the software version if it's a Novell print server, the number of printers serviced, the advertised name broadcast across the network for users to easily find, and the current server status. Choosing the current server status option allows you to take the server down immediately or after the current print job.

✦ **Users:** Users, groups, and containers are able to use this print server. Again, don't work with individual users for these types of items, use groups. Press Insert to add more users.

✦ **Operators:** Lists those users with authority over this Print Server. Press Insert to add more.

✦ **Description:** An optional field with room to type a line of print server description.

✦ **Password:** A handy security tool in case you have some users who wish to load the print server "inappropriately" according to the status message from Novell toward the bottom of the page.

✦ **Audit:** Some companies audit the use of everything. If your company does this, use this feature to track usage of the print server, and to set the location and size of the audit file.

Most of these options won't be used during normal administration. But when you need them, they're available through DOS with PCONSOLE, as well as within NWADMIN.

PRINTCON

PRINTCON (PRINT job CONfiguration) used to be much more painful than it is today. Printing is actually getting better, at least in little short steps, because printers are getting smarter. But configuring your default print job details must be done at least once.

Typing **PRINTCON** at a DOS prompt opens the program, and the Available Options menu lists three choices:

✦ **Edit Print Job Configurations:** Describes details, such as file contents (Byte Stream is the default), form feed or not, send notification when a print job is finished or not, the default printer and queue name, and whether you want to print a banner or not.

✦ **Select Default Print Job Configuration:** Different printers may demand different print job configurations, but one must be the default if the object needing print services doesn't specify one directly. Choose that print job configuration here.

✦ **Change Current Object:** Print jobs are configured by objects. You may configure a job for an individual user (although that's not the smartest way to spend your management time), group, or container.

If your network still includes Bindery servers, pressing F4 any time while viewing the main menu converts everything back to a format familiar to NetWare 3.*x* administrators.

PRINTDEF

Again, this program is in \PUBLIC waiting to be called from a DOS prompt. This utility adds controls for specific printers from the long list of PDF files shipped with NetWare, and lets you define printer forms for those printers.

PRINTDEF presents the following Available Options:

✦ **Print Devices:** You may Edit, Import, or Export print device printer files, which are tagged with the PDF extension. Editing a print device requires intimate knowledge of printer functions and control codes; avoid if possible.

✦ **Printer Forms:** Named forms, such as Legal or Letterhead, are handy ways to change printing characteristics when using different forms of paper. Your creation options are limited to the name, number of form, page length, and page width.

✦ **Change Current Context:** Standard context choice operations.

Printer definitions were a big deal when laser printers were new. Luckily, they are rarely needed today, because of all the new controls inside applications and Windows 95/98/NT that help format and control printed output.

NetWare User Stuff

Your users, luckily, don't see all configuration programs and utilities. However, some things they do need to see, which makes stuff easier for them to understand; therefore, you won't be bothered with so many questions.

Much of the initial hassle was taken out of client setup by the move from DOS and Windows 3.1 to Windows 95/98. This move required Microsoft and Novell to work more closely together, and both improved their client software.

Microsoft includes Novell client software with Windows 95/98/NT, but the software doesn't work well with NDS. However, it's better than it was; at first, Microsoft client software for NetWare networks ignored NDS altogether, forcing Novell to scramble and quickly get their own client software out the door.

Life with clients is a bit easier now, but still frustrating when there's a problem. DOS clients using NET.CFG files give you that warm, fuzzy feeling that you can tweak the settings when necessary, but the advanced interfaces today separate you from the controls. You're forced to use the Control Panel to reach the Networking properties, and sometimes that's not quite enough.

NetWare clients and configurations

The easiest way to install a few NetWare clients is by using the NetWare installation CD-ROM. When you start the CD-ROM, you're offered the choice of installing server or client software. All the files are on the CD-ROM disk, and the configuration details are minimal. The same process can be done by loading the CD-ROM files onto a NetWare server, to make it easy to upgrade clients.

Upgrading existing NetWare clients brings up another interesting option: Automatic Client Upgrade. This is a process rather than an application, but it automates the client upgrade process. To enable the Automatic Client Upgrade, perform the following steps:

1. Create a folder (directory) on the NetWare server. For example, from the root of your NetWare volume, type **MD ACU** from a DOS prompt.

2. Copy the NetWare client files and Windows Installation .CAB files into this folder.

3. Allow all users you're upgrading to have access to this new folder. For example: Open NWADMIN, right-click the \ACU directory, choose Details from the popup menu, and then click the Trustees of this Directory button. Click Add Trustee, and then choose the \ACU directory. Click OK to save and exit.

4. Update the NWSETUP.INI file for your client configuration changes.

5. Modify login scripts to automatically run the SETUP.EXE file in the new upgrade folder.

The only trick here is setting up the NWSETUP.INI file, and that's not difficult. Set the Version = setting, in the format of 3.0.0.0, for major version, minor version, revision, and level. Any increase in this number triggers a software upgrade.

In the [AcuOptions] portion of the NWSETUP.INI file, you must tell the system if you want to allow the users to choose whether or not to upgrade, and if they want to reboot the computer or not. If you set

```
DisplayFirstScreen=YES
```

users have a choice about whether to upgrade. Similarly, setting

```
DisplayLastScreen = YES
```

allows users to abort the automatic reboot process. It's your choice.

Configuration details are much the same for all the various levels of Client32 software (which all the software is today, and has been for awhile). For NDS clients, set these fields to match your network:

- ✦ Preferred Server
- ✦ Preferred Tree
- ✦ Name Context
- ✦ First Network Drive

For NetWare 3.*x* clients, set only the Preferred Server; the rest doesn't matter.

Changing Properties for a NetWare workstation with Windows 95/
98/NT can be done through Network Neighborhood or the Network
Control Panel. To do it through the Control Panel:

1. Open Control Panel, and then open Networking. (Select
Control Panel⇨Start menu⇨ Settings.)

2. Click Services⇨Novell Client⇨Properties.

3. Make the changes you wish, and then click OK.

4. Reboot if necessary.

Novell's Z.E.N.works offers new ways to change the configuration
Properties of multiple systems simultaneously. It can be valuable
in network setting. Ask your dealer about a trial version of
Z.E.N.works today. Also see Part V for more information about
Z.E.N.works.

Basic user commands and capabilities

Your users may wish to do a few more things, even after you set up
NetWare Application Launcher and set their Login Scripts to map
all the proper drives.

With Windows 95/98/NT, most network configuration comes from
within Windows. NetWare 5's client software can put an icon in
your Systems Tray, ready for a right-click and configuration at any
moment. Until you upgrade to NetWare 5, however, here are a few
things to teach your users:

✦ **Mapping drives:** Network Neighborhood offers a good
graphical interface. Browse your neighborhood until you find
the volume or directory you want. Right-click the chosen
object and choose Novell Map Network Drive from the menu.
Choose a drive letter for this connection. Save and exit.

✦ **Choosing a Printer:** Open Control Panel⇨Printers, and then
choose a networked printer icon. If one doesn't exist, choose
Add a Printer, and then pick a network printer or queue name
from the list that appears after you click the Network print
server radio button. If a network printer doesn't appear, call
the administrator. If you must add a driver to your Windows
system to utilize the chosen printer, choose the driver from
the long list offered by Windows after you click OK on the
message window that tells you your PC doesn't have a
suitable print driver installed.

✦ **Login to NetWare:** The NetWare Client32 software puts a
NetWare Login option in the Novell Program folder. If a user
wants to log in again with a different name, or to a different
tree, that user must provide his or her username and password, the tree name, the context, and the preferred server.

✦ **Change password:** Users may change their passwords by choosing Control Panel⇨Passwords⇨Change Other Passwords. They must provide the old password and type the new password twice for verification. Explain to these users that you can't help them find their password if they forget, without a lot of trouble, so they should remember theirs.

✦ **Capture a Printer Port:** Users need to go back to Network Neighborhood, right-click the printer or queue, and then choose Capture Novell Printer Port.

Details, such as file attribute settings and the rest, are more properly left to you, the administrator, although users may change their own if they wish. Have them study the documentation and show you that they understand before you let them start playing with file attributes, even in their own subdirectories.

Applications coordinate data sharing, not the users. Security and access controls can't be changed by the users themselves, or at least they shouldn't be. Turning curious users loose with a help key (F1) and the security clearance to change things will provide more excitement than you really want, so don't let the users do those things.

Part IV

NetWare Tools, Commands, and Minor Utilities

NetWare includes a vast number of minor utilities that you use to manage and maintain clients and servers. Throughout the following sections, we take a look at the majority of these minor utilities, how you use them, and what to watch out for.

In this part . . .

- ✔ Command-line syntax review
- ✔ Management utilities from the console
- ✔ Client-based file and directory management utilities
- ✔ Information-gathering utilities and commands
- ✔ Helpful keyboard shortcuts
- ✔ GUI utilities
- ✔ NetWare 3.*x*-specific utilities

Command-line Overview

Before you can use these utilities, you need to understand how we list them in the text. Whether you're doing so on the server's console or in a client's command window, the steps for using these commands are pretty much the same. After we introduce each command, we list the syntax for that command as follows:

Syntax: COMMAND *required parameter [optional parameter]*

The command itself appears in all caps, as does any other command that you need to use at the same time, such as LOAD. Remember that very few commands are case-sensitive. After the command, we list the types of parameters available for that command. Parameters appearing in brackets are optional. You press Enter after each of the commands to start the utility. The table that follows each line of command syntax, as the following example shows, outlines the available parameters for that command:

Parameter	Function
param1	The first available parameter.
param2	The second available parameter.

Console Management Utilities (Administrators Only)

The utilities that we discuss in this section are performed at the server's console. Because you're working directly with the server, you should use these utilities only if you're an administrator. And by all means, be careful!

ADD NAME SPACE

You use this command to add name-space support to a volume on a NetWare server.

Syntax: ADD NAME SPACE *[name [TO [VOLUME] volume_name]*

Prerequisite: Use the LOAD NAME SPACE name command to load the name space into memory before using ADD NAME SPACE. See LOAD for more information.

Parameter	Function
none	Displays the loaded name space modules.
name	The name space module to add to the volume. Options are MAC, LONG, NFS, and FTAM. FTAM is a third-party add-in.
volume_name	The volume to which you want to add the name space. For example, SYS.

BIND

You use this command to manually link a network protocol to a network interface. See INETCFG for information on automatically linking protocols to NICs.

Syntax: BIND protocol [TO] *LAD driver* or *board name* *[LAN driver parameter] [protocol_parameter]*

Prerequisite: You must load the LAN driver, such as 3C5X9.LAN, before you can use the BIND command.

Parameter	Function
protocol	The protocol that binds to the card. Usually IPX or TCPIP.
LAN_driver	The driver for your LAN card.
board_name	After you load the LAN driver, you may name the entry if you want (for example, LOAD 3C5X9 FRAME=ETHERNET_II NAME=TESTING). You can use that name here rather than that of the LAN driver.
LAN_driver_parameter	Any driver parameter that applies to your configuration, such as FRAME (Ethernet frame type) or INT (also known as IRQ).
protocol_parameter	Any parameter specific to the protocol. For example, an IPX network number or an IP address and subnet mask.

CD

In NetWare 3.12 and 4.*x*, you use this command to manage a CD-ROM that you've mounted as a NetWare volume.

Syntax: CD *parameter [option]*

Prerequisite: You must load the CD-ROM NLM before you can use the CD commands. See LOAD for more information on loading NLMs.

Parameter	Function
help	Displays information on available parameters and options for the CD utility.
mount	Mounts a CD-ROM disc as a volume. Some available options are ALL and /R, which you use to rebuild the index of the CD-ROM.
device list	Displays a list of the CD-ROM device drivers that are on the server.
volume list	Displays a list of the CD-ROM discs currently mounted as volumes.
dismount	You guessed it! This parameter dismounts a disc so that it is no longer a NetWare volume and so you can remove it from the server.
change	Dismounts the existing volume and then prompts you to insert the new disc. After the disc is in the drive, press Enter, and the new CD is mounted as a volume.
rename	You can't have two volumes with the same name in a NetWare server, but on certain occasions, two CDs may have the same name. Use rename to change the name of one of the CDs on the NetWare server. Remember, however, that you must dismount the volume before you can rename it.
DIR	Displays a list of the directory contents on the root of the CD-ROM. To use DIR, you must dismount the volume.
group	You use group to combine CDs into logical groups if you have more than one CD-ROM drive in your system. Just typing **CD GROUP** displays the groups defined on the server.
purge	Purges the index files created when a CD volume is mounted. Index files take up space on your SYS volume. Purging these files forces the system to reindex volumes as they mount, but doing so saves space.

CLEAR STATION

The CLEAR STATION utility enables you to clear a particular client connection to the server. This utility is very handy if you must perform network maintenance and people don't log off the server.

Be careful in using this utility. If you clear a client's connection while it is saving data to the server, the data is lost.

Syntax: CLEAR STATION *station number* or *ALL*

Parameter	Function
station number	The connection number as displayed in MONITOR or through NLIST. See MONITOR and NLIST in this part.
ALL	Just as it says — everybody on the server.

CLS

This command clears the screen on the console.

Syntax: CLS

CONFIG

This command displays the server's configuration, including file server name, IPX internal network number, server up time, LAN driver and network information, NDS tree name, and bindery context.

Syntax: CONFIG

CONLOG

This utility keeps a log of everything that happens on the console screen and saves it to a file. This utility is especially helpful if you're troubleshooting a remote server, because you can have someone send you the file to take a look at what's going on. The filename is CONSOLE.LOG and it resides in the SYS:\ETC directory.

Syntax: LOAD CONLOG [file=] [save=] [maximum=] [entire=]

Parameter	Function
file	The filename to which you want to save the new log.
save	The filename to which you want to save the existing log.
maximum	The maximum size in kilobytes of the log file.
entire	Captures the lines that are already on-screen as you load CONLOG. Otherwise, CONLOG starts logging when the next line appears.

DISABLE LOGIN

You use this utility to prevent users from logging in to the server. DISABLE LOGIN is another handy utility if you have network maintenance to perform, such as a backup or repairing a volume.

Syntax: DISABLE LOGIN

DISMOUNT

DISMOUNT removes a volume from service so users can't access it. You must DISMOUNT a volume before you can perform most maintenance, including repairing the volume using VREPAIR.

Be careful when using this utility. Just as with other commands, if you DISMOUNT a volume while users are writing data, they could easily lose the data.

Syntax: DISMOUNT *volume_name*

Parameter	Function
volume_name	The name of the volume you want to dismount.

DISPLAY ENVIRONMENT

This utility enables you to view the operating environment for the server. The information it displays includes the server's search path, protocol settings, and NDS settings.

Syntax: DISPLAY ENVIRONMENT

DISPLAY NETWORKS

This utility provides a list of networks that are visible from the server and is particularly handy if you're troubleshooting communication problems between clients and servers on multiple networks.

Syntax: DISPLAY NETWORKS

DISPLAY SERVERS

Similar to the DISPLAY NETWORKS utility, DISPLAY SERVERS lists the servers that the local server knows about via broadcasts. Also, like DISPLAY NETWORKS, it's very useful in troubleshooting communication problems between servers on a network.

Syntax: DISPLAY SERVERS

DOMAIN

Use this early NetWare utility (2.x, 3.x, and 4.0) to load an NLM in a protected area of memory for testing. Using DOMAIN, which is actually an option of LOAD, an NLM that's acting up can run and crash without taking down the entire server. Since the introduction of IntranetWare, however, this NLM is no longer available.

Syntax: LOAD DOMAIN

DOWN

This utility is perhaps one of the most often used utilities in NetWare. Using DOWN is much like closing up shop at the end of the day. It gracefully closes all network connections, dismounts the volumes, shuts down the system, and, in NetWare 5, automatically returns you to DOS. (In other versions of NetWare, you must use the EXIT command to return to DOS.) Of course, if you use this utility while users are accessing the server, you could end up with some pretty unhappy campers on your network.

Syntax: DOWN

Before bringing your server down, use SEND or BROADCAST to inform the users that the server is going down. Also use CLEAR STATION and DISABLE LOGIN to ensure that all users have "left the building." Thank you. Thank you very much.

EDIT

As you may imagine, you use EDIT to edit files, particularly NCF files or plain-text files. This utility, however, has few of the extensive features you've come to know and love from such stunning applications as MS-DOS's EDIT. You can block text and move or delete it from the file fairly easily using the function keys. (Press F1 after loading for a full explanation.)

Syntax: LOAD EDIT *filename*

ENABLE LOGIN

The exact opposite of DISABLE LOGIN, you use this utility to enable users to connect to the server. After any network maintenance, make sure that you re-enable logins, especially before you go home for some well-deserved rest.

Syntax: ENABLE LOGIN

EXIT

EXIT is used in pre-NetWare 5 versions to return to DOS after the server has been taken down. This utility is especially handy if you're testing a server, because you don't need to go through an entire reboot; you just rerun SERVER.EXE after returning to DOS. Of course, if you opt to use REMOVE DOS (see the section on that utility, later in this part), you have nothing to which to return, and so EXIT reboots the server.

Syntax: EXIT

FILTCFG

You use this utility to control the way the routing features of NetWare operate. You can use FILTCFG to create filters for IPX, TCP/IP, AppleTalk, and Source Route Bridging.

Although this utility seems like a cool function, limiting the way protocols operate can create rather large problems on your network, such as servers not seeing each other.

Syntax: LOAD FILTCFG

Prerequisite: You must enable filtering support through INETCFG before filters you create can become active.

Option	Available Filters
IPX	**Global IPX Logging**
	Outgoing SAP Filters
	Incoming SAP Filters
	Outgoing RIP Filters
	Incoming RIP Filters
	NetBIOS and Packet Forwarding Filters
TCP/IP	**Global IP Logging**
	Outgoing RIP Filters
	Incoming RIP Filters
	Outgoing EGP Filters
	Incoming EGP Filters
	OSPF External Route Filters
	Packet Forwarding Filters
AppleTalk	**Device Hiding Filters**
	Outgoing Route Filters
	Incoming Route Filters
Source Route Bridge	**Protocol ID Filters**
	Ring Number Filters

HALT

You use this very specialized command only on mirrored SFT III servers. You use this command to bring down an IOEngine. Needless to say, if you need this command, you're going to know it. Most people don't need it.

Syntax: HALT

HCSS

You use this utility on pre-NetWare 5 servers to view the settings and commands that you use in the NetWare High Capacity Storage System. The safest way to manage an HCSS volume is by using the NetWare Administrator and not the console commands. A few of the many HCSS parameters are described here; for more information, check the NetWare online documentation.

Syntax: HCSS *parameter = setting*

Note: HCSS parameters are case-sensitive, and you should use them only with extreme caution. In NetWare 5, NSS replaces HCSS.

Parameter	Function
none	Displays a list of HCSS parameters and their settings.
Eject Media Override	Keeps jukebox media from being ejected.
Delete Through	Specifies the method for notification for file deletions. If set to off, the files immediately go in the delete queue. If set to on, you receive notification of a successful deletion only after the deletion is complete, which is more secure.
Migrate Unarchived Files	Determines whether files with their archive bit on migrate to the HCSS volume.
Migrate Compressed Files Only	Determines whether only compressed files or files that you can't compress migrate to the HCSS volume.
Minimum Time In Drive	The number of seconds a side of media can remain active before it is traded for another side (jukebox operations).
Maximum Time In Drive	The opposite of Minimum Time In Drive; the maximum number of seconds that a side of media can remain active before being switched for another side.
Request Idle Time	The number of seconds HCSS waits before switching one side of media from the drive for another. The idle time begins after the Minimum Time In Drive expires.
Migration	Turns migration on or off.

HELP

Your best friend, this utility displays information about all console commands.

Syntax: HELP *command name*

INETCFG

You use this utility to configure all your networking parameters. Its options are enormous and include selecting all the configuration parameters for each of your network cards and all the protocols. One very important thing to remember, after you run INETCFG, the utility remarks out network card and protocol settings in the AUTOEXEC.NCF and uses a number of .CFG files instead. You *must not* delete or edit these files manually — use INETCFG only.

Syntax: LOAD INETCFG

INSTALL

For versions of NetWare other than NetWare 5, you use this utility to manage the configuration of your server, including mirroring or duplexing drives, formatting a hard disk, configuring devices, adding licenses, changing or creating volumes, and modifying the main NCF files. In NetWare 5, NWCONFIG replaces this utility. (See the NWCONFIG section, later in this part.)

Syntax: LOAD INSTALL

IPXCON

You use this utility to monitor IPX routing services on a server. Using IPXCON, you can track general IPX information, such as number of packets sent and received by the server, IPX routing information, address mapping information, circuit information, services information, and NLSP information.

Syntax: LOAD IPXCON [/P]

Parameter	Function
/P	The only parameter available for IPXCON. You use it to view the LSPs that the router receives if the remote router is running NLSP.

IPXPING

You use this utility to check the connectivity between the server and another device on the network, usually a server or client computer. The catch here is that you must know the network number and node address of the destination for IPXPING to work.

Syntax: LOAD IPXPING

After you load IPXPING, enter the network number, node, and node address of the computer you want to ping. You can also specify the seconds to pause between pings and the size of the packets to send. After all your information is correct, press Esc to begin pinging.

KEYB

You use this utility to tell NetWare what type of keyboard you're using. As you can probably guess, keyboards vary greatly from country to country. In NetWare 5, the following keyboard types are available: Belgium, Brazil, Canadian French, Denmark, France, Germany, Italy, Japan, Latin America, Netherlands, Norway, Portugal, Russia, Spain, Sweden, Swiss French, Swiss German, United Kingdom, and the United States.

Syntax: LOAD KEYB *[keyboard_type]*

Parameter	Function
none	Displays the list of available keyboard types.
keyboard_type	The type of keyboard you are using.

LANGUAGE

This utility works closely with KEYB. You use it to define the language that system modules use. The utility, however, applies only to modules that you load *after* the command. So, if you're running your NetWare server in a country other than the United States or you just like to read in French, make sure that you add this command early in your AUTOEXEC.NCF file.

Syntax: LANGUAGE *[language_name* or *number]* [LIST] *[REN number new_name]*

Prerequisite: You must install the language modules on your server *before* you can switch languages. You install modules in the SYS:SYSTEM\NLS*language_number* directory. See the list of languages for their associated number.

Parameter	Function
none	Displays the current language setting.
language_name	The name of the language to use.
number	The predefined language number.
LIST	Displays all defined language ID numbers and their names.
REN number new_name	Allows you to change the name of a language. For example, you might change *French* to *Francois* by typing *REN 6 Francois*.

Language Number	Language Name
0	French-Canadian
1	Chinese-Simplified
2	Danish
3	Dutch
4	English
5	Finnish
6	French-France

(continued)

Language Number	Language Name
7	German
8	Italian
9	Japanese
10	Korean
11	Norwegian
12	Portuguese-Brazil
13	Russian
14	Spanish-Latin America
15	Swedish
16	Chinese-Traditional
17	Polish
18	Portuguese-Portugal
19	Spanish-Spain
20	Hungarian
21	Czech

LIST DEVICES

Guess what! This command displays the devices that connect to your server, such as CD-ROM drives, disk drives, or any other device with a driver.

Syntax: LIST DEVICES

LIST STORAGE ADAPTERS

Similar to the LIST DEVICES command, this utility displays a list of the storage adapters configured on your server. This list looks very much like the LIST DEVICES list.

Syntax: LIST STORAGE ADAPTERS

LOAD

The granddaddy of all console programs. You use this utility to load NLMs on the server. You always use it in conjunction with an NLM, such as IPXCON or MONITOR. The parameters that you use depend on the NLM that you're loading.

Syntax: LOAD *command*

MEMORY

A nice, simple, straightforward utility, MEMORY displays the amount of memory in your server. Good if you can't remember, but bad if you realize that you need more RAM.

Syntax: MEMORY

MEMORY MAP

This utility tells you how much memory, in bytes, DOS and the server are using. Really, it tells you how much DOS is using and that the server is using everything else.

Syntax: MEMORY MAP

MIRROR STATUS

On a server where you're using mirroring or duplexing, this utility displays the status of the mirrored partitions on your server. This utility is very handy for determining whether a mirrored partition is working correctly or, after replacing a drive in a mirrored partition, whether the resynchronization is complete.

Syntax: MIRROR STATUS

MODULES

Displays a list of all modules on the server, including NLMs, DSKs, and LANs.

Syntax: *MODULES [string]*

Parameter	Function
none	Displays all loaded modules.
string	Displays a list of modules matching the entered string. MODULES I*, for example, displays only those modules with names that begin with *I* (IPXSPX.NLM, INETLIB.NLM, and so on).

MONITOR

MONITOR is one of the most useful utilities available on a NetWare server. Get to know it and come to love it. It displays vital system information about the server, such as CPU utilization, number of connected users, and server up time. And that's all just on the first screen! The following figure shows the main MONITOR screen for NetWare 5. The options that you get are different if you're using another version of NetWare. After a few seconds of inactivity, the top box in MONITOR expands to include more real-time information, such as current disk requests and current open files.

Selecting one of the options in the bottom half of the screen
enables you to further manage and configure the server. Selecting
Connections from the Available Options menu, for example,
displays a list of all users logged in to the server and their
connection numbers. If you select a particular user from that list
and press Enter, you see a list of the files that user has open. If
you press Delete instead, you can clear the user's connection. As
always, be careful what you do to users!

From the Available Options area of the main MONITOR screen, you
can view storage device configurations and information on
volumes, LAN/WAN drivers, loaded modules, open and locked
files, disk-cache utilization, system resources, virtual memory, and
kernel performance. Finally, you can modify certain server
operating parameters.

In NetWare 5, none of the switches that earlier versions of NetWare
used are valid. The parameters defined in the table are for earlier
versions of NetWare.

Syntax: MONITOR *[parameter]*

Parameter	Function
/p	Includes processor information that is not normally available in MONITOR.
NS	Turns off the screen saver that MONITOR uses.
NH	Turns off the Help screens available through MONITOR.

MOUNT

You use the MOUNT utility, the opposite of DISMOUNT, to initialize
an existing volume for use by clients.

Syntax: MOUNT *volume_name* or ALL

Parameter	Function
volume_name	The name of the specific volume you want to mount.
ALL	Mounts all volumes configured on the server that currently aren't mounted.

NAME

This simple command displays the name of the server, which is most helpful if you're walking into an operations center with many, many servers. Of course, placing a label on the server, keyboard, or monitor usually helps too.

Syntax: NAME

NCUPDATE (4.x only)

You use this utility to automatically configure users' NET.CFG files after you move or rename a container. Place the command in a login script to ensure that the users' configuration files update.

Syntax: NCUPDATE [/?] [/VER] [/NP]

Parameter	Function
/?	Displays a Help screen.
/VER	Displays the version of NCUPDATE and the associated Unicode files.
/NP	Sets the utility so it updates the NET.CFG without prompting for user input.

NMENU (4.x) or MENU (3.x)

These utilities enable you to make menus from which your DOS clients can work. Using these utilities enables you to control how users enter applications and what they can do on the network. Windows systems replace these applications with the NetWare Application Launcher in IntranetWare, which comes with the new Z.E.N.works utilities for NetWare 5.

Syntax: NMENU

NSS

NSS is the newest high-performance storage system for NetWare. As with HCSS, the majority of the configuration and monitoring options are available through other utilities, such as the NetWare Administrator or NWCONFIG. A few command-line options, however, are available for NSS.

Syntax: NSS *option*

Parameter	Function
help or /?	Displays the Help screen for NSS and its associated NLMs.
version	Displays the NSS version information.
modules	Displays information about all modules involved in the NSS system.
status	Displays statistical information about the NSS system, such as buffer size and cache percentage.
menu	Invokes a menu that enables you to view and configure NSS volumes.

NVER

You use this pre-NetWare 5 utility to view version information for the various components of NetWare, including the version of DOS, the version of NetWare, and LAN driver information.

Syntax: NVER *[/C] [/?] [/VER]*

Parameter	Function
/C	Continuously scrolls the information across the screen instead of stopping at the end of each screen and waiting for you to press a key.
/?	Displays Help information.
/VER	Displays the version number of the NVER utility and its associated components.

NWCONFIG

In NetWare 5, NWCONFIG replaces INSTALL, but it performs much of the same functions, including managing configurations for disk drives and volumes, NSS disk options, licenses, and NDS options. The following figure shows NWCONFIG.

Syntax: [LOAD] NWCONFIG

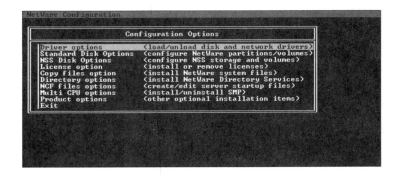

Menu Option	What You Can Do
Driver options	Configure, load, and unload disk and network drivers.
Standard disk options	Configure and modify partitions, mirrors, and volumes.
NSS disk options	Configure and modify NSS volumes.
License option	Add or remove NetWare client licenses.
Copy files option	Install the NetWare system files from CD.
Directory options	Install or remove directory services or import a 3.*x* bindery into NDS.
NCF file options	Create or modify your AUTOEXEC.NCF or STARTUP.NCF files.
Multi CPU options	Install or remove SMP modules.
Product options	Install, view, or configure other NetWare products, such as Distributed Print Services.

NWXTRACT

This is another utility that is no longer available in NetWare 5. You use NWXTRACT to decompress NetWare files from the CD-ROM or floppy disks onto the file server.

Syntax: NWXTRACT *path filename or groupname [destination] [/option]*

Parameter	Function
path	The path to the master data file FILES.DAT.
filename	The name of the file that you want to extract.
groupname	The name of a group of files that you want to extract. The groupnames are available through online Help.
destination	The location to which you want to extract the files.
/s=server	Instructs NWXTRACT to copy the files to their normal location on a particular file server.
/t=type	The type of files to extract, such as MAC, DOS, OS2, and so on.
/?	Displays the Help screen.
/VER	Displays the version number of the utility and its associated files.

OFF

This utility works the same as CLS. It clears the console screen, plain and simple — nothing else.

Syntax: OFF

PING

This utility works just as IPXPING does, except that it uses TCP/IP rather than IPX to check the connectivity between computers.

Syntax: LOAD PING

After you load the application, you must supply the IP address or host name of the computer you want to ping. You can also specify the number of seconds between pings and the size of the IP packet that you want to send.

PROTOCOL

This utility displays the protocols installed on the server and also registers additional protocols or frame types. Most often, however, the configurations that you establish by using this command are better off set through INETCFG or NWCONFIG.

Syntax: PROTOCOL *[REGISTER protocol frame ID#]*

Parameter	Function
none	Displays the protocols registered on your server.
REGISTER	What you use to register a new protocol on the server.
protocol	The name of the protocol to register.
frame	The frame type that the protocol uses (for example, Ethernet_802.2).
ID#	A unique hexadecimal number that you use to identify the protocol to the server.

RCONSOLE

This utility is one of the most useful available from NetWare. It enables you to look at the server console from another computer on the network.

Syntax: RCONSOLE *[servername] [servername*]*

Prerequisite: You must load REMOTE and RSPX on the server before you can use RCONSOLE.

After you load RCONSOLE, you are prompted to select the type of connection you want to use (asynchronous or LAN). Select the type of connection, and you'll see a list of available servers. Select the server with the console you want to control and enter the password when prompted.

You need to remember the following points when dealing with RCONSOLE:

✦ If another administrator is working on the console and is typing or changing screens, these things could affect the work you're doing.

✦ Because RCONSOLE is character-based, it doesn't handle the new NetWare 5 server-based GUIs very well, so try to keep from viewing that screen.

✦ Use Alt+F1 to display the RCONSOLE Help screen.

✦ Use Alt+F2 to exit RCONSOLE.

✦ Use Alt+F3 and Alt+F4 to cycle between screens on the server.

Parameter	Function
servername	The name of the server that you want to control.
servername*	The partial name of the server that you want to control.

REGISTER MEMORY

Use REGISTER MEMORY on NetWare 3.*x* and 4.*x* servers to enable the server to recognize memory higher than 16MB.

Syntax: REGISTER MEMORY *start_address amount*

Parameter	Function
start_address	The hexadecimal address of the top end of the memory currently registered on the server. Usually, the top end is 1000000h, or 16MB. To obtain the start address for your server, run the MEMORY command and convert the number to hexadecimal.
amount	The amount of memory to register with the server. This number is also written in hex, so have fun!

For more information on converting decimal to hexadecimal, refer to your high school math or science books.

REMIRROR PARTITION

You use this utility to begin the remirroring process for a particular partition. Most often, remirroring occurs automatically. You may, however, face some instances in which you must take the controls yourself and tell the server exactly what to do: "Sit. Stay. Remirror partition. Good server."

Syntax: REMIRROR PARTITION *partition_number*

Parameter	Function
partition_number	Yup, it's the partition number of the logical partition that you want to start remirroring.

REMOTE

This NLM loads on the server console to support remote management through RCONSOLE. Without loading REMOTE, RCONSOLE
doesn't work.

Syntax: LOAD REMOTE *password* or -E *password*

Parameter	Function
none	A prompt appears that asks you to supply the password that enables you to access the server. Type carefully, because the password doesn't appear on-screen. If you do goof up, you can always unload and then reload REMOTE.
password	Instead of prompting you to supply a password, the utility uses the password that you enter on the command line.
-E password	If you use this option, you must encrypt the password that follows.

To create an encrypted password, follow these steps:

1. Load REMOTE normally and supply a normal password.

2. On the console, run **REMOTE ENCRYPT** and supply a password when prompted.

You receive an encrypted password to use when connecting
via RCONSOLE and the utility asks you whether you want to
use this password.

3. Write the password down and double-check it.

The encryption process turns a nice, short word (such as
austin) into a huge hexadecimal string (such as
BFC893609D55A5AFADD2C). If you can't remember this
string, however, you can still use the original password you
entered at the time that you loaded REMOTE.

REMOVE DOS

In all versions before NetWare 5, this utility removes the DOS
operating system from memory to give more memory to the
server. If you use this command, the server reboots after you type
EXIT, instead of returning to DOS. This command is not necessary
in NetWare 5 and, therefore, is not available.

Syntax: REMOVE DOS

RESET ENVIRONMENT

You use this utility to return changed SET values (such as Default Tree Name) to their default setting. After issuing the command, a prompt asks you whether you want to change each individual setting, all settings, or to quit the utility.

Syntax: RESET ENVIRONMENT

RESET ROUTER

RESET ROUTER clears the routing information from the server and rebuilds the tables. This command is useful if you've had a router or server crash and need to make sure that all the servers and routers have the same information.

Syntax: RESET ROUTER

RESTART SERVER

This handy little troubleshooting tool saves you a couple steps in the shutdown/restart sequence. Instead of requiring you to type **DOWN**, then returning to DOS (either automatically in NetWare 5 or by using EXIT in all other versions), and then typing **SERVER** at the DOS prompt, this utility performs all these tasks for you.

Syntax: RESTART SERVER [-parameter]

Parameter	Function
-ns	Restarts the server but doesn't run the STARTUP.NCF or AUTOEXEC.NCF files.
-na	Restarts the server but doesn't run the AUTOEXEC.NCF file.

SCAN FOR NEW DEVICES

This interesting little utility scans the system for new devices and registers those devices with the media manager. This utility is most often used after you add a new device that requires special drivers to be loaded before the system can recognize the device, or when dealing with hot-swappable equipment, such as hard drives.

Syntax: SCAN FOR NEW DEVICES

SCRSAVER

If you've worked with earlier versions of NetWare, you're familiar with the famous "red-snake" screensaver that was part of MONITOR. Well, this screensaver now has its own utility — and a lot more versatility. For example, the screensaver can now operate on screens other than MONITOR, including the GUI ConsoleOne.

Using the settings that the parameter table describes, you can determine how many seconds of inactivity triggers the screensaver and whether the console locks as the screensaver activates.

Syntax: SCRSAVER [option1 [option2] [option3]

If you're using multiple options, separate them using semicolons, as follows: SCRSAVER DELAY=300; ENABLE LOCK; AUTO CLEAR DELAY=25.

Parameter	Function
help	Displays the list of available SCRSAVER options. You can also use SCRSAVER HELP command_name to get help on a specific parameter.
status	Displays the current configuration of the screensaver. The figure that appears after the table shows an example of how this configuration may appear.
activate	Starts the screensaver immediately instead of waiting for the prescribed seconds of inactivity.
auto clear delay	The number of seconds the unlock screen appears before automatically returning to the screensaver. The default is 60 seconds.
delay	The number of seconds without keyboard or mouse input before the screensaver activates. The default is 600 seconds (10 minutes).
disable	Hmmmm? Disables the screensaver? You got it.
disable auto clear	If you use this option and the unlock screen activates, the unlock screen doesn't clear away from the screen.
disable lock	If the server receives input from either the keyboard or the mouse after the screensaver starts, this option immediately returns you to the console without requiring a password.
enable	You guessed it: This option enables the screensaver to operate.
enable auto clear	Removes the unlock screen after a certain number of seconds. This is the default setting.
enable lock	After the screensaver is active, if you press a key, you must enter a password to gain access to the console. You must use an Admin user or an equivalent user to unlock the screensaver. This is the default setting.

The following figure shows the status of the screensaver after you enter the settings for it.

```
REAL_MACHINE:scrsaver status
    Screen saver enabled: Yes
    Lock screen when saved: No
    Delay before saving screen: 300 seconds
    Automatically clear unlock portal: Yes
    Delay before clearing unlock portal: 60 seconds
REAL_MACHINE:_
```

SEARCH

You use this utility to modify the server's search path, which the server then uses to locate a file instead of requiring you to always specify a file's location. Can you imagine needing to type **SYS:SYSTEM** before every command that you execute on the server?

Syntax: SEARCH [ADD [number] path] or DEL [number]

Parameter	Function
none	Displays the current search-path settings.
ADD	Adds the search path setting that you define after you type the parameter itself. Pretty self-explanatory, huh?
number	Defines the number of the search path setting (for example, Search 1, Search 2, and so on). The order of the search path defines where the server looks for files first.
path	Defines the location of the new search path.
DEL	Deletes the specified search path.

SECURE CONSOLE

You use this utility to further enhance the security features of NetWare. The SECURE CONSOLE command is used to restrict the types of actions that can be performed on the server console or through RCONSOLE. For example, after the console is secure, you can load modules only from directories that are already in the search path, and the search path can't be modified. As an additional enhancement, no one can load modules from a DOS partition, even if the partition is in the search path. Finally, the server's date and time cannot be modified; this ensures that Directory synchronization stays on track.

One cautionary note: After you use SECURE CONSOLE, the only way to unsecure it is to reboot the server.

Syntax: SECURE CONSOLE

SEND (also BROADCAST)

You use this utility to send text messages from the server console to all users on the network or to specific users. The BROADCAST command performs the exact same functions and can be used interchangeably. This capability is very, very handy if you need to take a server down for maintenance and you want to warn your users. A nice message, such as File server MARTIAN will be taken down in 15 minutes; please log off, is preferable to one such as Get off the server or lose your data!

Syntax: SEND "message" [logon_name or connection_number] [AND logon_name]...

Parameter	Function
"message"	The text of the message that you want to send. The message must be less than 55 characters long. Quotes around the message are necessary only if you're not sending the message to all users.
logon_name	The logon name for the user to whom you want to send the message.
connection_number	The connection number for the user to whom you want to send the message.

SERVER

The first utility you need to use, SERVER is the program that brings your NetWare server into being. You run it from a DOS prompt, and it initializes the server for use.

Syntax: SERVER parameter

Parameter	Function
-ns	Starts the server but doesn't run the STARTUP.NCF or AUTOEXEC.NCF files.
-na	Starts the server but doesn't run the AUTOEXEC.NCF file.

SERVMAN

You find SERVMAN in NetWare 4.x and IntranetWare only. You use this utility to view and configure some of the server's settings. In the Server parameters section, for example, you can use it to

modify the SET commands that appear in the AUTOEXEC.NCF
and STARUP.NCF files. SERVMAN also provides real-time information
on server performance, such as server up time and volume
information. In NetWare 5, the MONITOR program performs these
functions.

Syntax: SERVMAN

SET

This utility is another with which you're sure to become very
familiar. You use it to view and establish the operating parameters
of the server. To turn file compression on and off, for example, you
use SET ENABLE FILE COMPRESSION. Many variables are
available for this command — enough, in fact, for a book all its
own. Needless to say, we don't have enough room here to cover
this information.

Syntax: SET [parameter]

Parameter	Function
none	Enables you to view the current system settings. Settings are grouped into categories, such as File system or Disk. Choose the category that you want to view from the list that appears.

SET TIME

This particular SET parameter is so important that it gets its own
listing. As you may guess, you use it to set the time on the server.
But guess what? You also use it to set the date! Amazing little
utility, don't you think?

Syntax 1: SET TIME hh:mm:ss am/pm

Syntax 2: SET TIME mm/dd/yy hh:mm:ss am/pm

Syntax 3: SET TIME mm/dd/yy

SPEED

This utility displays the speed rating of your CPU. For example, on
our test server, which is a Pentium 233 MHz, we get a reading of
12243. The utility bases the speed not only on the CPU's clock
speed (233 MHz), but also on the type of processor (Pentium) and
the number of memory wait states.

Syntax: SPEED

TCPCON

As is true of IPXCON, you use TCPCON to monitor the performance of the TCP/IP protocol suite. The main screen displays the number of IP and TCP packets that the system sends and receives. Using the list of available options for the utility, you can manage SNMP access to the server, view and modify protocol settings, view and modify the IP routing table, view protocol and interface statistics, and view the local trap file.

Syntax: TCPCON

TIME

Displays the server's time and date information, including timezone and time-synchronization settings.

Syntax: TIME

TRACK OFF

The exact opposite of the following command, TRACK OFF turns off router tracking. So what is router tracking? Read on, fearless reader, read on.

Syntax: TRACK OFF

TRACK ON

This utility is very useful for troubleshooting in that it tracks the routing packets that are passed between servers and routers. Even better, it tracks connection requests from clients. Say, for example, that you're having problems getting a client to connect to a server. If you know the MAC address of the client, you can turn on tracking and watch the connection requests. Pretty neat, huh?

Syntax: TRACK ON

UIMPORT

You actually run this utility on a workstation and use it to import large numbers of users into NDS automatically. If, for example, you're installing a new NetWare server and you already have all the employees' names and other information in a database, you can export the database to a plain-text file and then import the user information into NetWare. In NetWare 3.*x*, MAKEUSER performs this function, but it works the same way.

Syntax: UIMPORT *control_file data_file* [/C] [/?] [/VER]

Parameter	Function
control_file	The name and location of the control file you're using. A control file defines the fields in your data file, as well as their order.
data_file	The actual information from your database that defines the user's account.
/C	By default, UIMPORT pauses after each screen of data. Use this parameter to continuously scroll through the output.
/?	Displays Help information.
/VER	Displays the version of UIMPORT and its associated files.

UNBIND

You use this utility to manually break the link between a protocol and a network interface card. You most often use it if a protocol has an incorrect configuration that you need to change or to stop network traffic for a particular protocol.

Syntax: UNBIND *protocol* [FROM] *LAN_driver* or *board_name* [*LAN_driver_parameter*]

Parameter	Function
protocol	The protocol that you want to unbind from the card.
LAN_driver	The LAN driver for your interface card.
board_name	The name that you assigned the LAN driver when you loaded it.
LAN_driver_parameter	Any driver parameter that specifies the instance you want to unbind. For example, your network may be using IPX on both the 802.2 and 802.3 frames. You can unbind only one instance at a time, so you can specify which one to unbind using this information.

UNLOAD

Hmmmm, could this utility possibly unload drivers and programs such as MONITOR? You got it. See LOAD for more information.

Syntax: UNLOAD *NLM name* or *application*

VERSION

This utility displays the version and license information for the NetWare installation on your server. It's pretty handy if you happen to forget how many licenses you've installed.

Syntax: VERSION

VIEW

Quite simply, this utility enables you to view, but not edit, files on the server, such as the AUTOEXEC.NCF. Make sure that you enter the full path to the file, because VIEW doesn't use the server's search path.

Syntax: VIEW *path\filename*

VOLUME (S)

Whether with or without the *s*, this utility displays information about the volumes you have mounted on your server.

Syntax: VOLUME[S] *[volume_name]*

Parameter	Function
none	Displays information on all mounted volumes on the server, including volume name, the name spaces enabled on the volume, and the flags associated with the volume.
volume_name	Displays detailed information about the specific volume, including the number of blocks it uses, the total number of blocks on the volume, the data streams on the volume, the name spaces, and the flags.

VREPAIR

VREPAIR is an extremely useful utility. You use it to fix problems with volumes, such as damaged files or screwed-up directories. To ensure the integrity of your data, you should always use it after your server crashes. Did we mention that it's a useful utility? In NetWare 4.*x* and 5, if the server detects serious problems with a volume, it runs VREPAIR automatically.

Syntax: LOAD *[path]* VREPAIR

Parameter	Function
path	The location of the VREPAIR NLM.

Imagine a server with a single volume (SYS). Because of some unknown force (possibly poltergeists), a crash occurs. Upon restart, you find that the SYS volume is damaged and it won't mount. But, if SYS doesn't mount, how do you load VREPAIR?

The solution is one that many of us picked up the hard way. No matter which version of NetWare you're running, make sure that the VREPAIR.NLM file is on your DOS partition in the same directory as SERVER.EXE. By doing so, you can load VREPAIR even if SYS is damaged. Because Novell realized how important this solution is, NetWare now automatically copies VREPAIR (and many other important NLMs) to the DOS partition.

File and Directory Utilities

The utilities that we discuss in this section you run from a client workstation command prompt and use to view and configure files and directories, as well as to navigate the NDS tree.

ATTACH (NetWare 3.x only)

Back in the dark ages before NDS, a user had to log in to each server individually. Imagine! You did so by logging in to one server normally and then using the ATTACH utility to connect to the other server. If you use ATTACH and don't supply a fileserver name or user name, you see a prompt asking you to do so.

Syntax: ATTACH [fileserver_name or user_name]

Parameter	Function
fileserver_name	The name of the server to which you want to connect.
user_name	Your login name on the server.

CX

CX is an NDS navigation tool that you use to view or change your context. It's especially useful on DOS-based clients. If your network still includes DOS or Windows 3.11 clients, you'll become very familiar with CX.

Syntax: CX [new context] [/option...] [/?] [/VER]

Parameter	Function
new context	The area of the Directory tree to which you want to move.
/R	Displays containers at the root level or changes context in relation to the root.
/T	Displays container objects at the current context and below.
/CONT	Displays container objects at the current context.
/A	Displays *all* objects and not just container objects.
/C	Continuously scrolls the output instead of pausing at the end of each page.
/?	Displays Help information.
/VER	Displays the version of CX on the server.

FILER

FILER is a character-based file manipulation tool. Its roots lie in the early versions of NetWare, when the program had no File Manager and moving files by hand in DOS was time-consuming and tedious. Several options are available from the main FILER screen, which we discuss in the table following the syntax. The tool really has only one command-line option: /VER, which displays the version information of the program.

Syntax: FILER [/VER]

Menu Option	What You Can Do
Manage files and directories	Enables you to modify or view files, add or remove directories and subdirectories, view or modify rights to files and directories, and view trusts for files and directories.
Manage according to search pattern	Enables you to view the file and directory lists based on a search pattern.
Select Current Directory	Enables you to set your current context, volume, and directory.
View volume information	Displays volume information, such as owner, creation date, volume type, and total kilobytes available.
Salvage deleted files	Enables you to view and retrieve deleted files that NetWare has not yet purged from the server.
Purge deleted files	Enables you to remove deleted files from the server.
Set default filer options	Enables you to set the default options for the way FILER operates, including confirmation settings and how it manages file attributes.

FLAG

This handy little command-line utility enables you to change a file's attributes. If you're familiar with DOS, FLAG is the same as the ATTRIB command but easier to work with.

Syntax: FLAG *file or directory [+ or - attribute]*
[/option] [/?] [/VER]

Parameter	Function
none	Displays the file attributes for all files in the directory.
file or directory	The object with the attributes that you want to modify.
+ or –	Indicates to the utility whether you're adding or removing an attribute.
attribute	The file or directory attribute that you want to change. The attribute could be Ro, for *Read Only*, for example, or A for the *a*rchive bit.
/NAME = name	Sets the ownership for a file or directory to the specified username.
/GROUP = name	Same as NAME = but sets ownership to a group of users.
/D	Provides detailed information for the files listed.
/FO	Stands for *Files Only*. Displays only file information and not directory information.
/OWNER = name	Lists the files with the specified ownership.
/M = mode	Enables you to modify the search mode for executable files. You probably don't want to mess with this one.
/S	Enables you to search subdirectories below the current directory.
/C	Continuous display instead of stopping at the end of every page.
/?	Displays Help information.
/VER	Displays version information.

MAP

This is another utility with its roots in the pre-Windows 95 era. You use MAP to assign drive letters to volumes on the server so applications can address them. Of course, users are more likely to remember that their files are "on the F: drive," which is a shorter name, than at DATA:USERS\HOMEDIRS*myname*.

Syntax: MAP [P] [NP] *[option] drive:= [drive: or path]* [/?] [/VER]

Parameter	Function
none	Displays your current mapping information.
P	A new addition with NDS; you can specify a connection to a physical volume rather than a volume object. Must be either the first or second option listed.
NP	If you use this option and tell map to overwrite an existing mapping, it doesn't prompt you before doing so. Must be either the first or second option listed.
C	Changes a search drive to a regular drive or vice versa.
DEL	Deletes a drive mapping.
INS	Inserts a search drive without replacing an existing mapping.
N	Uses the next available drive letter instead of specifying a drive.
R	Maps a fake drive root. (See the Tip that follows this table for more information.)
W	Doesn't change the master environment.
drive:	The drive letter or mapping that you want to assign to the new path. Can be either a letter (R:=) or a search setting (S3:=).
path	The location to which you want to map a drive.
/?	Displays Help information.
/VER	Displays version information.

Of all the options available with MAP, R is probably the coolest. It's really handy if you have an application — say, maybe an e-mail package — that expects data files to be in a particular directory, such as M:\EMAIL. Of course, most network administrators shiver at the thought of installing data files directly off the root of a volume. So, using the R option, you can fake the application into thinking that M:\EMAIL is really the root simply by using a command such as the following: MAP R DATA:APPS\INTERNET. (This example assumes, of course, that your e-mail package is actually installed at DATA:APPS\INTERNET\EMAIL.)

NCOPY

Just about everyone is familiar with the old DOS command COPY. You use it to copy files from one location to another. Well, Novell's done COPY one better with NCOPY (Network COPY — get it?). The cool thing about NCOPY is that it is *much* faster than COPY, especially when copying from one directory on a server to another. Even better, it retains all the file attributes that COPY just doesn't understand.

Syntax: NCOPY [source_path] filename destination_path [filename] [/option] [/?] [/VER]

Parameter	Function
source_path	The location from which you want to copy the file or files.
filename	The file that you want to copy.
destination_path	The location to which you want to copy the file or files.
filename (the second time)	If you want to rename the file as it copies, enter the new filename here.
A	Copies files with the archive attribute set and leaves the attribute on the source file turned on.
M	Copies files with the archive attribute set and turns off the archive attribute on the source file. Use this option to use NCOPY for backups.
C	Copies the file without retaining extended attributes or name-space information.
F	Forces the utility to copy sparse files.
I	Gives you a notification method if NCOPY can't retain extended attributes or name space information because the destination path doesn't support them.
R	Retains file compression.
/R /U	Retains file compression even if the destination doesn't support compression.
S	Copies subdirectories and their contents.
/S /E	Copies subdirectories, including empty subdirectories.
V	Verifies the copy by comparing the original file with the new file.
/?	Displays Help information.
/VER	Displays version information.

NDIR

NDIR outperforms DOS's DIR command. Just as with DIR, you use it to display file and directory information. NDIR, however, goes far beyond DIR in that it displays information such as attributes and ownership. You can use many parameters with NDIR. Some of the most important are covered in the parameters table that follows. For more information, use NDIR /HELP.

Syntax: NDIR [path] [/option...]

Parameter	Function
none	Displays the file and directory information for the current directory.
path	The path to the file and directory information you want to view.
HELP	Displays Help information.
SUB	Searches subdirectories. This parameter is different from that of DIR, which uses just /S.
VOL	Displays volume information.
SORT xx	Sorts the information according to the second parameter, where xx can be CR (creation date), AC (date last accessed), AR (date last archived), UP (last update), OW (owner name), or SI (file size).
DE	Displays file details.

NETUSER

NETUSER is the all-purpose DOS user tool for NetWare 4.*x* and 5, which replaces a number of utilities in earlier versions of NetWare. It enables you to print, send messages to other users, change your context, and change your password. NETUSER's GUI counterpart is the NetWare User Tools and performs the same functions.

Syntax: NETUSER

The different options available in NETUSER are pretty self-explanatory and easy to work with, as you can see in the following figure. For more information, refer to the online documentation.

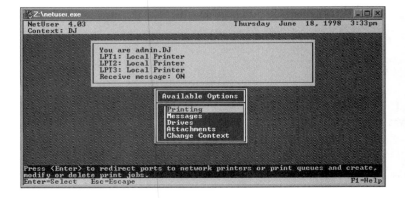

NLIST

You use this utility to view objects (such as users, groups, and printers) and search the Directory tree for objects. You also use NLIST to draw a map of your file and directory system. It replaces LISTDIR in 3.x. Although this utility was added in NetWare 4, you can use it to view Bindery objects on NetWare 3 servers.

The USERLIST command in NetWare 3.x was replaced by the NLIST USER command in NetWare 4.x and 5.

Syntax: NLIST [class type] [WHERE search option] [object name] [/option ...] [/?] [/VER]

Example: NLIST USER displays a list of all users who are logged in.

Parameter	Function
none or /?	Displays the first Help page.
class type	Inserts the specific object class you that want to view. Available classes include USER, SERVER, PRINTER, and GROUP. An * displays all class types.
search option	The operator that more specifically defines the list. For example, the command NLIST USER where "require a password" eq no provides you with a list of those users who don't require passwords.
object name	The name of the specific object with the information that you want to view. For example, use NLIST USER=SSONDHIEM to view information about Stephen Sondheim.
option	See the following table.
/VER	Displays version information.

Option	Function
/A	Lists all users who are logged in.
/B[=server name]	Lists the specified information from a Bindery server.
/C	Continuously lists the information instead of stopping after each screen.
/CO=	Defines the context that you want to search.
/D	Provides detailed information in the listing.
/N	Lists only the object's name.
/S	Searches all levels of the database beginning at the current context. Using this option is like searching subdirectories.
/SHOW[property]	Lists a specific property of an object, such as Require a password.
TREE	Lists all the trees available from this login.

PURGE

This utility does just what it says. It purges the current directory of deleted files. PURGE is very handy for freeing up disk space, particularly in older versions of NetWare. Be careful, however; after you run this command, the files really are gone. If you want to pick and choose which files to purge, use FILER instead.

Syntax: PURGE *[filename or path]* [/A] [/?] [/VER]

Parameter	Function
none	Purges all files in the current directory.
filename or path	Purges the specified file or files in the specified path.
/A	Purges all files in the current directory and all subdirectories.
/?	Displays Help information.
/VER	Displays version information.

RENDIR

At the time that NetWare was first introduced, this utility was one of the most useful around, and it still is today. You use it to rename directories. If you remember the old days of DOS, you couldn't rename a directory. You had to create a new directory, copy all the files over, and then delete the old directory. Well, this utility actually renames directories. And the really cool part is that you don't need to connect to the network to use it! It works all by itself, so you can copy it to your local hard drive and use it whenever you want.

Syntax: RENDIR *original name* [TO] *new name*

RIGHTS

This utility enables you to view or modify user and group rights to a file or directory. Most often, you use it to see who has rights to a particular file or directory before using the NetWare Administrator to assign new rights.

Syntax: RIGHTS *path* [[+ | -] *rights]* [/option . . .] [/? | /VER]

Parameter	Function
path	The path to the specific file, directory, or volume with the rights that you want to view or modify.
+ or -	Use it to add or remove specific rights.

Parameter	Function
rights	The specific rights, such as Read Only or Create, that you want to view or modify.
/C	Enables you to continuously scroll through the output instead of stopping at each screen.
/F	Displays the Inherited Rights Filter (IRF).
/I	Displays the information on who created the IRF.
/NAME=	The name of the user or group whose rights you want to modify.
/S	Enables you to view or modify subdirectories.
/T	Displays the trustee assignments for the current directory.
/?	Displays Help information.
/VER	Displays version information.

SETPASS

This utility is a very simple one that you use to change your password. If you have Administrator rights, you can even change someone else's password. Most often, passwords are changed through the NetWare Administrator.

Syntax: SETPASS [servername/] [username] [/VER]

Parameter	Function
none	Changes your password in the NDS database or on the current Bindery server.
servername	Changes your password on the specified server.
username	Changes the specified user's password.
/VER	Displays version information.

Information Commands & Utilities

Many of the utilities that we list in this section apply only to NetWare 3. You run them from a client computer and use them to gather information about the servers or the network.

CHKVOL (NetWare 3.x Only)

You use this utility to verify the status of your NetWare 3.x volumes.

Syntax: CHKVOL [volume_name]

Parameter	Function
none	Displays information about all volumes in the server.
volume_name	Displays information on the specified volume.

SLIST (NetWare 3.x only)

You use this utility to display a list of servers on the network. It's handy if you can't remember the exact name of the server to which you want connect to or if you think that a server may be down.

Syntax: SLIST [servername] [servername*]

Parameter	Function
none	Displays a list of all available servers. Using this parameter is pretty much the same as using the DISPLAY SERVERS command on the console.
servername	Lists the specified server.
servername*	Enables you to specify a partial server name to list (for example, SYST*).

VOLINFO (NetWare 3.x only)

VOLINFO enables you to look at the amount of space left on a volume and the volumes you can access.

Syntax: VOLINFO

WHOAMI

WHOAMI is the ultimate utility if you forget who you are. It displays your login name, the server to which you're connected, and your connection number.

Syntax: WHOAMI [option]

Parameter	Function
/ALL	Lists your effective rights, groups, security equivalencies, the people you manage, whether you're a workgroup manager, and other information.
/G	Lists the groups you're in.
/O	Shows the names of the users and groups you manage.
/R	Lists your effective rights.
/S	Shows your security equivalencies.
/W	Shows who you manage.

Parameter	Function
/C	Continuously scrolls through the output.
/?	Displays Help information.
/VER	Displays version information.

Keyboard Shortcuts

In this section, we dedicate a little space to how you use the keyboard with NetWare utilities.

Standard utility keystrokes

The following table lists the standard utility keystrokes.

Keystroke	Function
Esc	Exits a program from the main menu, discontinues a process, or returns to the previous menu.
Ctrl+PgUp	Goes to the beginning of a list.
Ctrl+PgDn	Goes to the end of a list.
Yes	"Okay, go ahead and confirm or exit."
No	"Nope, don't do what I told you to do."
PgUp	Goes to the top of the screen.
PgDn	Goes to the bottom of the screen.
Up	Moves to the preceding selection or line.
Dn	Moves to the next selection or line.
Ctrl+←	Moves to the beginning of the preceding word.
Ctrl+→	Moves to the next word.
Backspace	The universal key to erase the character to the left of the cursor.
Ctrl+Alt+Del	Reboots your workstation if all heck breaks loose.
Ins	Shows a list of options you can select from.
Del	Deletes an option that you previously selected.
Home	Goes to the beginning of the line.
End	Goes to the end of the line.

NetWare all-purpose editing keys

The following function keys you use in many of the NetWare menu utilities.

Key	Function
F1	Shows Help screens.
F3	Edits an entry.
F5	Marks an entry to delete items.
F6	Marks selections.
F7	Cancels changes you made.
F8	Unmarks marked selections.
F9	Changes modes.
Alt+F10	Exits from a menu utility.

Moving around the file server console

If you're stymied at the file server console, these two simple keystroke combinations get you around.

Keystroke	Function
Ctrl+Esc	Accesses the list of active programs.
Alt+Esc	Cycles from session to session.

The rule of the first letter

NetWare uses a first-letter rule to help you get around its menu utilities: If you enter the first letter of the selection you want, NetWare takes you to the selection. If numerous selections begin with the same letter, enter the first two letters or as many as necessary to specify a unique string.

NetWare GUI Utilities

With the advances in GUI operating systems, many of the NetWare utilities have been migrated to GUI as well. Perhaps the most important GUI utilities are the NetWare Administrator (NWADMIN) and NetWare User Tools that are discussed in Part III.

ConsoleOne

ConsoleOne is the cool new utility that you can use to manage your network. It's just like NWADMIN in a lot of ways, except that it's Java-based and runs on the server console rather than on a workstation. Aside from the fact that it runs on the server console, ConsoleOne is also different from NWADMIN in that you can use it only to manage users, groups, organizations, and organizational units. ConsoleOne also enables you to manage volumes on the server and the server's NCF files. In addition to the management capabilities of ConsoleOne, it provides tools that enable you to monitor the performance of the server. Because ConsoleOne is Java-based, it can run on any platform, enabling you to manage your NetWare server from whichever system you choose.

This stuff represents a very new and emerging technology. For more information on ConsoleOne, refer to its documentation.

NetWare Application Launcher (NAL)

In IntranetWare (NetWare 4.11), the NetWare Application Launcher enables you to provide easy access for your users to specific applications, much the same way NMENU worked in earlier versions. In NetWare 5, the NAL comes with the new Zero Effort Networks (Z.E.N.works) product, but its function is still the same. These utilities rely on objects created through the NetWare Administrator. For more information on creating objects, refer to Part III.

To set up NAL, follow these steps:

1. Create application objects in the NDS database that specify exactly where the application is located and how you access it. For more information, see Part III.

2. Assign specific applications to users or groups by using the Application area of the user's or group's properties.

Executing NAL is as simple as point and click. It reads the user's configuration from the NDS database and presents the applications to which the user has been granted access.

For more information on Application objects and NAL, refer to the online documentation.

NLS Manager

You use this utility to manage Novell licenses on a server — not only NetWare, but also other Novell programs. NetWare 5 stores the NLS Manager program in the SYS:PUBLIC\WIN32 directory. Once you've opened the application, you have the ability to view all Novell licenses in your NDS tree a number of different ways. Choose the different options through the View menu to determine how your licenses appear on the screen. In addition, you can create a License Usage Report by selecting this option from the Action menu. This creates a graphical report that outlines the number of licenses used versus the number of licenses installed for a particular product.

NetWare 3.x Menu Utilities

In all fairness, we should mention a few of the utilities that are available only in NetWare 3.x, so here they are.

COLORPAL

You should avoid the COLORPAL utility unless you have a bachelor's degree in fine arts. This utility enables you to change the colors of your soothing NetWare menus to colors that you may see in a psychedelic art gallery.

Syntax: COLORPAL

SALVAGE

SALVAGE is the catchall command that you need to use if you erase a file on a NetWare 3.x server that you really didn't want to erase. SALVAGE gives you several options: You can look at all the files you deleted, recover files that were deleted, or put files back in the directories they occupied before you erased them.

Syntax: SALVAGE

SESSION

SESSION enables users to move around from directory to directory without requiring explicit DOS commands for manual directory changes. If you must jump around directories often, SESSION may prove just the thing for you to use.

Syntax: SESSION

SYSCON

NWADMIN's predecessor, SYSCON is the NetWare control center for versions before 4.x. If you're a user, you can see all the information about yourself, which groups you're in, and your effective rights. If you don't have supervisor rights, you see only information about yourself.

Syntax: SYSCON

Integrating NetWare and Windows NT

Perhaps one of the most important tasks facing administrators today is integrating NetWare and Windows NT. With the tools available from Novell and Microsoft, getting these two competitors to work together is actually very easy, believe it or not!

Why integrate? Because Windows NT has become the application server of choice for many companies, relying on NT to support Web, e-mail, and database applications. Yet these NT systems run on company networks controlled and supported by NetWare. Both sides must work together if your company expects to get any work done.

In this part . . .

- ✔ **Examining Novell's integration utilities**
- ✔ **Examining Microsoft's integration utilities**
- ✔ **Discussing migration options**

Part V

Integrating from the Novell Side

The majority of Novell's integration options are client-side options that allow all Windows operating systems to connect to NetWare servers. In addition to some third-party utilities that perform similar functions, Novell has created NetWare Directory Services (NDS) for NT, which lets an administrator add a Windows NT Server to an NDS tree.

Installing Z.E.N.works and client components

With NetWare 5, Novell has expanded client support to include IPX connections for DOS and Windows 3.1*x* and both IPX and IP connections for Windows 95 and 98 and Windows NT 4. Novell's new Z.E.N.works (Zero Effort Networking) provides many client-management tools and utilities that make managing a large network easier.

You can find the client software on the Z.E.N.works CD-ROM, which you can purchase from Novell for approximately $39. The following example guides you through the client installation for a Windows 95 machine. The steps are similar for each of the other client types.

To install the Novell client software, follow these steps:

1. Insert the Z.E.N.works CD-ROM in the client workstation.

2. If the Autorun feature is enabled on your computer, the initial Z.E.N.works dialog box is opened automatically. If not, select Start⇨Run and click Browse. Locate your CD-ROM and double-click WINSETUP.EXE.

3. Click the appropriate language (in our case, English), and think New Age thoughts during the sound effects.

4. You are presented with a list of available installation options, including installing Z.E.N.works on the server, installing the documentation, and installing the client software for Windows 95, Windows NT, and Windows 3.*x*. The following figure shows the opening page.

5. As you move your mouse over each of the options, a description appears on the right-hand side of the box. Click Windows 95, which brings up a list of Windows 95 components. Your options are to install the client software, install the client documentation, install Netscape, install Win2NCS, and install the Java runtime. For more information on the items that you don't recognize, refer to the online documentation.

6. Click Install Novell Client. This action launches the installation program and quiets the sound effects.

7. You are first presented with the licensing agreement. Unless you don't want to install the software, click Yes.

8. The Welcome to the Novell Client for Windows 95 Install dialog box opens, as shown in the following figure. This dialog box gives you the option of a typical installation or a custom installation. Usually, a typical installation is fine. But for those of us who like to live on the edge, custom installation is the way to go. Select the Custom option and click Next.

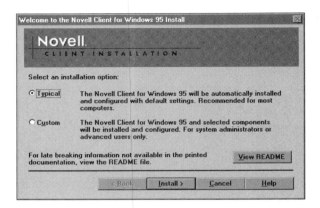

9. Next, select the protocol option your network uses. With NetWare 5, you have the option of running a pure TCP/IP network, a network with both TCP/IP and IPX, or a network with only IPX. You should have already made this decision, so pick the protocol option that fits your network and click Next. (We picked IPX.)

10. You're given the option of making an NDS connection or a Bindery connection. In most cases, you're going to want to make an NDS connection, so select it here and click Next. Only make a Bindery connection for NetWare 3.*x* network connections.

11. You also have the option of installing a number of other components. The following figure shows you your options. Select the additional components you'd like to install, click Install, and off it goes.

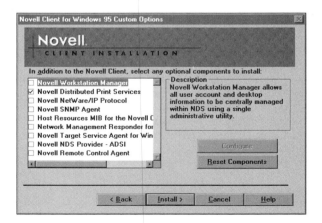

12. If the protocol(s) you decided to use is not already installed on the system, you see a prompt that instructs you to insert the Windows 95 installation CD-ROM. Do so and click OK.

13. After the files have been copied to your system, a dialog box appears that asks whether you want to configure your preferred server or NDS tree and context settings now. We suggest you choose Yes and finish the configuration, or the user will have to do it the first time he logs in.

14. If you clicked Yes in Step 13, you see the Novell NetWare Client Properties dialog box, as shown in the following figure. Enter the appropriate information for your server and choose a first network drive (usually F:); then click OK. The more information provided now, the easier for the user later.

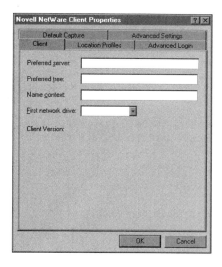

15. When the installation program finishes copying files, click Reboot and wait for the system to return.

After your computer reboots, you can log on to the NetWare server and the computer. Right-click the N on the right-hand side of the Taskbar to perform many network-related tasks. The following figure presents the menu you see when you right-click. Selecting NetWare Properties from the menu invokes a dialog box that enables you to change the settings for the NetWare client.

Integrating NT Domains and NDS

The most daunting task that faces administrators in heterogeneous networks (those with both NetWare and NT) is user and group management. Although the available client software provides easy connection to both types of servers, you must add user and group information to each system separately. To address this administration nightmare, Novell has introduced NDS for NT, which enables NT Servers to be added to a NetWare NDS tree. This addition means that the NT Server acts as a member of the tree just like any other server.

NDS for NT is not included with NetWare 5. You must purchase it separately. However, you can obtain a trial version from the Novell Web site (www.novell.com/download). Remember, never install trial software on a production server.

Before you start the installation, be sure that you are logged in to your Windows NT Primary Domain Controller Server as the Administrator or an equivalent user. To install NDS for NT, perform the following steps:

1. If you have purchased NDS for NT, insert the CD-ROM into the Windows NT Server. If the Autorun feature is enabled on your server, the NDS for NT installation program launches automatically. If not, or if you downloaded the trial version, open Explorer and double-click WINSETUP.EXE.

2. The main dialog box provides two options: Install NDS for NT and Install NDS for NT Administration Utilities. We talk about the Administration Utilities later in this section, so for now, click Install NDS for NT.

3. The NDS for NT Installation dialog box opens, welcoming you to the NDS for NT Installation. Click Continue.

4. You are then presented with the Novell Software License Agreement. Read through the agreement and then click Yes to continue. (Clicking No aborts the install.)

5. The installation program copies the files to the appropriate locations and reviews the Registry settings. When this process is complete, you are prompted to reboot the computer. Click Yes and wait.

6. When the NT Server has rebooted, press Ctrl+Alt+Del to log on. The Novell IntranetWare Client Services for Windows NT dialog box opens, allowing you to enter the tree and context information to which you're adding the server. This will be the home network for this server, and the information will be remembered the next time the system reboots.

7. On the Login tab, enter the NetWare username and password for the NDS tree. You can also specify the context to which you want to connect. Use the IntranetWare tab to locate a specific tree and context. When you finish entering this information, click OK.

8. After the system has completely restarted and you're logged in, the Domain Object Wizard is automatically launched. Click Next in the Welcome dialog box to continue with the installation.

9. The tree that you are currently logged into appears in the selection dialog box. If you want to add the server to another tree, select that tree now. Otherwise, click Next.

10. The next dialog box tells you that you must extend your schema. Click Next to extend the schema, and add some more functions to NDS to support the new NT Servers.

11. The next dialog box in the Domain Object Wizard enables you to specify the NDS context where you want to create the Windows NT Domain object and NDS User objects for users on the Windows NT Server. Enter the appropriate information (the container to hold the new NT additions to NDS) and click Next.

12. You need to decide whether you want the Domain Object Wizard to search your NDS tree for NT users. If you're absolutely sure none of your NT users have accounts on the NetWare server, you can skip this step. Otherwise, select I want to search for my NT users in NDS and click Next.

13. If you choose to search for users, you then need to pick which container to search. Click the Browse button, select the container to search, and click Next. If you choose not to search for users, jump ahead to Step 15.

14. Click the Search button to begin searching for duplicate users. When the search is complete, click Next to view the search results.

15. Whether you decide to search or not, you're presented with a list of the NT users, their action status (whether they'll be created in the NDS tree), and what the NDS username will be. Review the list to make sure you agree with the assessment and click Next.

16. Click Move to add the users, groups, and other objects to the NDS tree. When the move is complete, click Next.

17. That's it! It's over. You can view the log of the move or view the documentation from the last dialog box or you can just click Finish. When you click Finish, the NT Server reboots.

After you install NDS on the Primary Domain Controller (PDC) for your Domain, you must install NDS for NT on any Backup Domain Controllers (BDCs) to ensure they are updated correctly. Doing this again for the BDCs will go much more quickly, we promise.

Integrating on the Server-level

You can install the NDS for NT Utilities on the NT Server. These utilities modify the NetWare Administrator to support the new Domain Object that was created during the NDS for NT installation process. To install the utilities, log on to the Windows NT Server as Administrator and open WINSETUP.EXE, as we described in the previous section. Then select Install NDS for NT Administrative Utilities and follow these steps:

1. Read through and click Yes to accept the Software License Agreement.

2. Click Continue on the Welcome to the installation dialog box.

3. Review the Setup Selections, accept the defaults, and click OK to start the installation.

4. If you're prompted to overwrite newer files, we suggest clicking No.

5. After the installation is complete, you have the option of running the NetWare Administrator or closing the installation program. Selecting either choice finishes the installation.

Integrating from the Microsoft Side

Because Novell has historically had a large percentage of the networking market share, Microsoft has gone to great lengths to provide utilities to connect Windows NT 4.0 computers (both servers and workstations) to NetWare servers. Many of the utilities outlined in the following sections are included with the Windows NT 4.0 operating system. However, File and Print Services for NetWare

(FPNW) and Directory Services Manager for NetWare (DSMN) are part of Microsoft's Services for NetWare CD, which you must purchase separately. As we're writing this book, the Services for NetWare CD costs $149.

To use any of these utilities, you must be familiar with the Windows NT Control Panel and User Manager or User Manager for Domains. You also need access to the Windows NT CD-ROM or installation files and, if you're loading FPNW or DSMN, the Services for NetWare CD-ROM.

Gateway Service for NetWare (GSNW)

Gateway Service for NetWare (GSNW) is probably the utility that is used most often when connecting Windows NT Servers to NetWare servers. It enables Windows clients to connect to NetWare servers without loading additional client software (like Client32). It is loaded on the Windows NT Server and acts as a gateway between the clients and the NetWare server, converting requests and responses from the Microsoft network format to the NetWare network format and back again.

GSNW is installed as a service through the Network applet of the Control Panel. However, just installing the service isn't enough. After you install it, you must configure the NetWare and NT Servers to support the gateway. Also, you must install NWLink for GSNW to operate. If it's not installed already, it will be installed automatically when the service is installed. Follow these steps to install GSNW:

1. Log on to the Windows NT Server as Administrator or equivalent.

2. Open the Control Panel by choosing Start➪Settings➪ Control Panel.

3. Open the Network applet by double-clicking the Network icon.

4. The Network dialog box appears. Click the Services tab.

5. Click Add to invoke the Select Network Service dialog box, shown in the following figure.

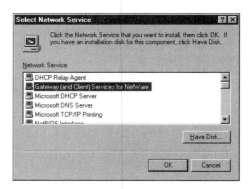

6. Select Gateway (and Client) Services for NetWare and click OK. We talk about Client Services for NetWare in the next section. For now, just know that installing GSNW also installs CSNW.

7. You see a prompt for the location of the Windows NT setup files. Usually, the location is the local CD-ROM drive (E:\I386). Make sure the location in the dialog box is correct and click Continue.

8. After the files are loaded and you're back at the Network applet, click Close to complete the installation. This step rebuilds the Registry and gets the NT system ready for reboot.

9. When the installation program is done configuring everything, you see a prompt that asks you to restart the computer. Click Yes, and wait for the computer to return to life.

After the system reboots and you log on to the NT Server, it will present you with the Select NetWare Logon dialog box, which enables you to specify which Bindery server (preferred server) or NDS tree and context to which you want to connect. This login process is actually a function of the Client Service for NetWare (which we discuss in the next section). The username that you're using to log on to the NT Server must exist on the NetWare server.

Because of the changes to the NDS database for NetWare 5, you cannot use the NDS tree and context settings to connect GSNW to a NetWare 5 NDS database. As of this writing, there is no new GSNW for NetWare 5, but we're sure there will be. Keep checking the Microsoft Web site (www.microsoft.com). If you're using GSNW and NetWare 5, you have to use a Bindery connection.

Now that you have GSNW installed, the next steps involve the NetWare server:

1. Using the NetWare Administrator, create a user that you will use to connect from the NT Server. (See Part II for more information about creating users.) We recommend a straightforward and easy-to-remember username like NT User. Set the user's password and don't let the user change the password. In addition, only allow the user to log in once. If you want to be absolutely sure that only the NT Server is logging in on this account, include a station restriction for the user. (For more information on how to do this, refer to Part VI.)

2. This step is recommended by Microsoft. Using the NetWare Administrator, create a group called NTGATEWAY. (See Part II for more information about creating groups.) Assign this group the permissions needed to access the resources on the NetWare server. These resources include files and directories, volumes, and printers. After assigning the appropriate access rights, add the user you just created to the new group. (See Part II for instructions on adding users to groups.)

As we mention, Microsoft recommends that you control access through the group NTGATEWAY. We have tested GSNW using a group name other than NTGATEWAY and have had no problems. We've also tested GSNW without a group by assigning the access permissions to the user directly and haven't had any problems.

By now, you may have guessed the biggest drawback to using GSNW. Every user who is granted access to the NetWare server through the gateway uses the same login name and has the same access. This permissiveness is due in no small part to Microsoft's theory on permissions: Grant full access to everyone first; then restrict as necessary. As you can imagine, you should plan your account strategy very carefully when using GSNW.

3. If it's not open already, open the Control Panel and double-click the GSNW icon. The Gateway Service for NetWare dialog box opens, as shown in the following figure.

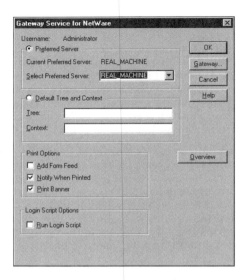

4. Click Gateway to configure the username and password that you created on the NetWare server. Doing so brings up the Configure Gateway dialog box.

5. Click Add in the Configure Gateway dialog box to create a share on the NT Server that identifies a resource on the NetWare server. The New Share dialog box appears.

6. In the New Share dialog box, create a share and click OK.

In the following figure, we've created a share called Data Volume that connects to DATA on the server REAL MACHINE. Note that you can limit the number of users accessing a particular share by selecting the Allow radio button and defining how many users in the list box. If you leave this setting as unlimited, every user with appropriate permissions who is logged on to the NT Server can be granted access to the NetWare resource.

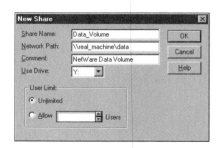

After you've created the share, you can change who has access to the share by clicking Permissions from the Properties dialog. By default, the group Everyone (which is slightly different in NT) is granted full control to the share. We recommend that you remove this permission and assign permissions to specific users or groups. Users and groups are created through the User Manager for Domains. For more information, refer to *Windows NT Networking For Dummies,* by Ed Tittel, Mary Madden, and Earl Follis (IDG Books Worldwide, Inc.).

Client Service for NetWare (CSNW)

Microsoft's Client Service for NetWare serves a single purpose: to connect Windows NT Workstation computers to NetWare servers. It provides Bindery connectivity to all types of servers and NDS connectivity to NetWare 4.*x* servers. Because of the changes to the NDS database with NetWare 5, however, it cannot be used to connect to a NetWare 5 tree. As of this writing, there isn't a newer version of CSNW that supports NetWare 5, but keep checking the Microsoft Web site. We're sure one will be out soon.

Installing the Client Service for NetWare is a simple process and is similar to installing other network services on a Windows NT computer. Note that CSNW requires NWLink to operate. If NWLink is not installed when the service is installed, it will be installed automatically. To install CSNW, follow these steps:

1. Log on to the Windows NT Workstation as Administrator or equivalent.

2. Open the Control Panel by choosing Start⇨Settings⇨ Control Panel.

3. Open the Network applet by double-clicking the Network icon.

4. Click the Services tab.

5. Click Add to invoke the Select Network Service dialog box.

6. Select Client Services for NetWare and click OK.

7. You see a prompt that asks you for the location of the Windows NT setup files. Usually, this location is the local CD-ROM drive (E:\I386). Make sure the location in the dialog box is correct and click Continue.

8. When the files are loaded and you're back at the Network applet, click Close to complete the installation. This step rebuilds the Registry and gets the computer ready to be rebooted.

9. When the installation program is done doing its duty, you are prompted to restart the computer. Click Yes and wait.

When the computer has restarted, initiate the logon process by pressing Ctrl+Alt+Del. After logging in to the NT system, you are presented with the Select NetWare Logon dialog box, which enables you to specify the Bindery server or NDS tree and context to which you want to connect.

For this process to work properly, the username must be the same on both the NetWare and NT Servers. The passwords don't have to be the same, but the usernames/login names do. This requirement is necessary because Windows NT automatically tries to pass the login information to the NetWare server when it's requested. If the login names aren't the same, you cannot connect to the NetWare server. This problem is fixed in the new NetWare clients section. For more information, see the Client32 section at the beginning of this part.

After the service is installed, you can modify its settings by opening the Control Panel and double-clicking the CSNW icon. Doing so pops up the Client Service for NetWare dialog box, as shown in the following figure. In addition to defining which server or NDS tree you're connecting to, you can specify how print jobs are handled and whether or not to run the login script when you attach to the NetWare server. Your choices for these options depend entirely on your network's setup.

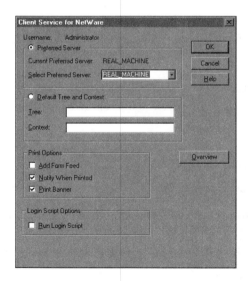

NWLink

NWLink is Microsoft's implementation of Novell's IPX/SPX protocol. It's completely compatible with IPX/SPX and is fully compliant
with all IEEE standards. Contrary to anything you might hear
regarding NWLink, it is not only used to connect to NetWare
networks, but it is also used very often to connect Windows
machines. Because IPX/SPX is routable, it's often a better solution
than the default Windows protocol, NetBEUI.

Installing NWLink is much like installing other network services or
protocols. Follow these steps to perform the installation on a
Windows NT Workstation (Windows NT Server and Windows 95
and 98 workstations use similar steps):

1. Log on to the Windows NT Workstation as Administrator or
   equivalent.

2. Open the Control Panel by choosing Start⇨Settings⇨
   Control Panel.

3. Open the Network applet by double-clicking the Network icon.

4. The Network dialog box appears. Click the Protocols tab.

5. Click Add and select NWLink IPX/SPX Compatible Transport.
   Click OK.

6. As always, you see a prompt that asks you to supply the
   location of the Windows NT setup files, which is usually the
   CD-ROM (E:\I386, for example). After you enter the appropriate path, click Continue.

7. The files are copied to their appropriate place on the server
   and you return to the Network applet. Notice that NWLink
   NetBIOS is added automatically when NWLink is installed.
   This happens because Windows NT Servers use NetBIOS
   names to identify computers on the network. IPX has no
   provision for this, so the NWLink NetBIOS protocol is added.

8. Click Close. The bindings are reviewed by NT and you see a
   prompt to restart the system. Click Yes and wait for the
   computer to be revived.

When the system is back up, you can communicate using NWLink.
You can access the configuration options by choosing the Protocols
tab in the Network dialog box. Select NWLink and click Properties.
(See the following figure.)

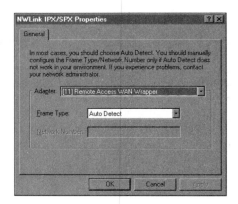

NT detects the frame type automatically. This option works well for networks using IPX over 802.2 or 802.3 frames. There have been some problems using autodetect with other frame types, such as Ethernet_II or Ethernet_SNAP. If you specify the frame type to use, you must also provide the IPX network number. You'll know things are working when you can see NetWare networks in your Network Neighborhood display.

When NWLink is installed on a Windows NT Server, additional options are available. These options include enabling routing, which provides a separate network number for each frame type and supplies the internal network number. Assigning your Windows NT Server a unique internal network number is very important. The default, which is assigned automatically when NWLink is installed, is 00000000. If you have more than one computer with this internal network number, communications will be impaired. If you're using NWLink on more than one NT server, be sure to change this setting by editing the display box and changing the network number.

File and Print Services for NetWare (FPNW)

File and Print Services for NetWare serves precisely the opposite function as GSNW. It allows NetWare clients to connect to a Windows NT Server without installing additional redirectors (client software). However, unlike GSNW, there is no gateway between the servers. The Windows NT Server advertises its services as if it were a NetWare 3.*x* (Bindery) server and accepts requests from NetWare clients. This service is particularly handy if you have clients running Windows 3.11 or DOS where memory is at a premium. It's also useful if you have non-Microsoft clients connected to your network.

Also, unlike GSNW, FPNW is not included with Windows NT Server 4. It is part of the Services for NetWare CD-ROM that you must purchase separately. When you have the CD-ROM, you add the service as you would add any other networking service (that is, through the Network applet of the Control Panel). Use the following steps to install and configure FPNW:

1. Log on to the Windows NT Server as Administrator or equivalent.

2. Open the Control Panel by choosing Start⇨Settings⇨ Control Panel.

3. Open the Network applet by double-clicking the Network icon.

4. Click the Services tab in the Network dialog box and click Add to bring up the Select Network Service dialog box.

5. Click Have Disk and enter the path to the Services for NetWare CD-ROM. Click OK.

6. The Install File and Print Services for NetWare dialog box appears. In the appropriate boxes, enter the name of the directory that will act as the SYS volume and the server name. Enter and confirm the password for the Supervisor account and determine the tuning option to be used. When the information is complete, click OK to continue.

- Microsoft recommends that the directory for the SYS volume be located on an NTFS volume so all NetWare access permissions can be assigned to the files and directories. If the directory is placed on a FAT partition, no file-level access permissions can be assigned. During the installation process, the NetWare 3.*x* directory structure (MAIL, LOGIN, PUBLIC, and SYSTEM) is added to the specified path. In addition, the PUBLIC directory is populated with NetWare commands, such as MAP and CAPTURE.

- The server name by default is the computer's name with FPNW appended (such as MYSERVER_FPNW).

- The Supervisor account is automatically added to the User Manager for Domains, along with an account for the service itself (FPNW Service Account) and the Console Operators group account. The Supervisor is also automatically added to the Administrators local group on the NT Server.

7. A prompt asks you to supply a password that the File and Print Services will use for NetWare service. Enter a password that you can easily remember and click OK.

8. Click Yes when you see a prompt to reboot the system.

The FPNW service modifies the User Manager for Domains to include NetWare login information. Use the Maintain NetWare Compatible Logon option to ensure that users are granted access to the NT resources. Remember that users created this way must also be created on any NetWare servers on your network to provide connectivity. This process does not automatically synchronize logins. The Directory Services Manager for NetWare takes care of automatically synchronizing logins.

Directory Service Manager for NetWare (DSMN)

The Directory Service Manager for NetWare is not included with Windows NT, but rather, like FPNW, is part of the Services for NetWare CD-ROM that you must purchase separately. DSMN synchronizes login names and passwords from a Windows NT Server to one or more NetWare 3.x servers. Because it accesses the Bindery for the servers and not the NDS database, it should not be used to synchronize accounts with NetWare 4.x or 5 servers.

You install DSMN, like other networking services, through the Network applet of the Control Panel. Before you install DSMN, you must install GSNW. See the GSNW section for installation instructions. Follow these steps to install and configure DSMN:

1. Log on to the Windows NT Server as Administrator or equivalent.

2. Open the Control Panel by choosing Start⇨Settings⇨ Control Panel.

3. Double-click the Network icon.

4. In the Network dialog box, click the Services tab and click Add to bring up the Select Network Service dialog box.

5. Click Have Disk and enter the path to the Services for NetWare CD-ROM. Click OK.

6. A prompt asks you to provide and confirm the password for the account that runs the Directory Service Manager for NetWare. The installation program automatically creates the SyncAgentAccount on the Windows NT Server, which operates the service. Provide the password for this account here.

7. If you installed FPNW before installing DSMN, you get a dialog box telling you that accounts created with the Maintain NetWare Compatible Login option may not be propagated to the other server. Click OK.

8. The Select NetWare Server dialog box opens. Select, from the list, the server with which you want to synchronize account information and click OK.

9. At the prompt, you supply a username and password with which to connect to the NetWare server you selected. Generally, you should use the Supervisor user, but a user with equivalent rights works too. Enter the information and click OK.

10. The Propagate NetWare Accounts to Windows NT Domain dialog box opens, and it enables you to specify a number of different synchronization options. These options include the following:

- Whether the user must change his password the next time he logs in

- Whether Supervisors should be added to the Administrators group

- Whether File Server Console Operators should be added to the Console Operators group

- Whether a mapping file should be used or, if not, a list of the users and groups to be migrated

- How passwords are automatically assigned (none, password is username, password is a specific word, or password is randomly generated)

When the information in this dialog box has been entered, click OK.

11. Finally, the installation program prompts you to make a backup of the Bindery using BINDFIX. We strongly recommend that you do this because there is always a chance that something will go wrong. Click Yes to perform the synchronization.

From this point, you should add any user that needs to be added to the network through User Manager for Domains, not through SYSCON. When users are added, they are automatically propagated to the NetWare server.

Migration Options

Although each of the utilities described in this part is designed to ease the integration of Windows NT and NetWare, you may encounter occasions in which only one type of server can be used. The following sections outline the migration options between Windows NT and NetWare.

From NetWare to Windows NT

When the two types of servers just can't get along, get out the Migration Tool for NetWare from Microsoft.

✦ It copies the file system and much of the user and group information from a NetWare server to a Windows NT Server.

✦ It enables you to select which files and directories to copy over to the new system because you really won't need the PUBLIC directory anymore.

✦ It even has a trial migration feature that gives you an idea of what's going to happen before you actually run the migration.

✦ It also includes extensive reporting so you know exactly what happened.

This utility is useful if you have to make the switch, but you need to remember quite a few caveats:

✦ The Windows NT Server must have GSNW and NWLink loaded, and make a backup before proceeding.

✦ To maintain access permissions, the destination volume on the NT Server must be formatted as NTFS. FAT won't do.

✦ Not all user information is transferred. Because passwords are encrypted, they cannot be read by the migration utility.

✦ All users must be logged off of both servers to ensure the migration is successful.

When you have both servers prepped and ready to go, use the following steps to migrate from NetWare to NT:

1. On the Windows NT Server, log on as Administrator or a user with equivalent permissions.

2. Click Start➪Run and enter NWCONV.EXE in the dialog box. Click OK.

3. The Select Servers for Migration dialog enables you to specify the NetWare server you are migrating from and the NT Server you are migrating to. Enter the server names or browse the network by clicking the ellipsis (...). After you enter the server information, click OK.

4. The Migration Tool for NetWare dialog box opens. Click User Options to define how usernames, groupnames, and passwords will be handled. The password options are:

• No Password

• Password is Username

• Password is (which makes all users' passwords the same)

When you're done defining the user and group options, click OK.

5. Back in the Migration Tool for NetWare dialog box, click File Options to define which files are moved and how NetWare volumes are created on the NT Server. After you've finished defining these options, click OK.

6. Again back in the Migration Tool for NetWare dialog box, you have two migration options: Start Migration or Trial Migration. We recommend running a trial migration and reviewing the logs before running the actual migration. When you're sure everything is ready to go, click Start Migration to transfer the NetWare server to the NT Server.

After the migration is complete, restart your server and test some of the users that were migrated. Verify that the passwords you specified for the users are working and that the permissions transferred correctly.

From Windows NT to NetWare

No utilities are available today to migrate from Windows NT Server to a NetWare server. Novell's approach seems to be that you can easily configure a NetWare server to work together with a Windows NT Server, including sharing usernames and passwords, network resources, and network management duties. If you must migrate from Windows NT to NetWare, we recommend you get in touch with Novell by calling 1-800-NETWARE. There are tools for migrating large NT installations to NetWare, but they remain the property of the Novell consulting services group.

Part VI

Common Administrative Tasks

The tasks in this part we call "common" for a good reason — every administrator must perform them, every network needs for someone to do them, and they're not particularly outstanding. Or, if truth be told, exciting — but you must take care of them.

Think of the tasks that you perform to maintain your network as you think of the tasks that you perform to maintain your car. The good part is that you don't need to crawl under a dirty engine. See — this stuff doesn't sound nearly as awful now, does it?

In this part . . .

✔ **Using the NetWare Administrator utility**

✔ **MONITORing your network server**

✔ **Repairing damaged NDS trees**

✔ **Installing new servers more quickly than before**

✔ **Making print arrangements**

✔ **User and group administrative functions**

Basic Administrative Tasks

The majority of tasks that you must perform come from the jobs that the majority of people using your network do every day — such as accessing files, printing, coming, going, changing jobs, communicating, and trying to get away with things. Hence, our administrative tasks tend to be "fun" things, such as those involving file- and directory-access settings, printer control, network communications, and security.

Technically, anything the administrator does with the network is an administrative task. That's why we label this part *common* administrative tasks. Some things you do on a network rarely, if at all — which is good, because the unusual tends to be problematic. The idea here is to help you cover your day-to-day network management tasks, which leaves plenty of time for planning ahead and avoiding those heart-stopping, late-night emergencies.

Browsing in NetWare Administrator

We cover the basics of NetWare Administrator in Part III, but here we want to go a bit deeper and point out some extra ways to get a better graphical grip on your network. NWADMIN enables you to open multiple windows at once, and you should take advantage of this capability to drill down into your network and display parts of your network in more detail.

Open the appropriate NWADMIN program for your management workstation, and one window opens automatically. This window displays your current context (location within the NDS tree), so the actual display can vary if your workstation changes contexts during the day.

Of course, computer screens display more information horizontally, whereas hierarchical displays work vertically. So open many windows displaying short containers that fit on one screen rather than one long container that you must scroll back and forth to see.

You can easily open another browser window by following these steps:

> Right-click a container or volume, and choose Browse in the pop-up menu that appears.

Or:

> Highlight a container or volume, and click the Browse icon on the toolbar.

Or:

> Highlight a container or volume and then choose
> Object⇨Browse from the main menu bar.

You can adjust browser windows by "grabbing" the edge with the
mouse pointer and dragging the window into the shape you want.
You can use the icons on the toolbar to cascade or tile the various
open browser windows.

Do whichever you prefer, but make sure that you know how to
open more than one window to avoid endlessly scrolling up and
down a long tree display. If we knew how to lay the tree on its side,
we'd tell you. Until then, use your Browser tools to your advantage
whenever possible.

Handling trustee rights

A *trustee* is a network object that has some control over another
object, hence you "trust" it with this authority. The [Public] object
in NDS, which is similar to the Everyone group in NetWare 3.*x*,
grants all users and groups certain trustee rights for objects that
everyone uses, such as printers and the SYS:PUBLIC directory.

Granting trustee rights may be simple, but the implications are
often considerable.

✦ Do users in your network need the authority to change login
scripts?

✦ Do they have the rights to all the files and directories they
need for their job?

These types of changes are relatively minor ones for NDS. Changes
must ripple through the NDS database, but doing so doesn't take
too long for such a small change. These changes take effect almost
immediately.

Some common changes to trustee rights are ones that you make to
files, directories, or even entire NetWare volumes. These rights
you normally grant to a group of some type, such as a user group
or a container that's holding users. To change trustee rights,
follow these steps:

1. Open NWADMIN from the appropriate Windows-equipped
workstation.

2. Double-click the Container, Group, or User objects to receive
these new rights.

3. Click the Rights to Files and Directories button.

4. Click the Show button to open the Select Object dialog box
pick list.

5. Double-click the volume in which the object in Step 2 is to have more or fewer rights.

6. If you want to grant rights to directories or files, click the Add button and then move through the Select Object dialog box until you find the directories or files to which you want to grant those rights.

You may select multiple items by holding down the Control key while you click.

7. Click OK to save the list of rights that you're granting.

8. Highlight the file or directory in the Files and Directories window and then change the Rights underneath by marking or clearing the check boxes next to the rights that you want to modify.

9. Click OK to save and exit.

You can change these rights for individual users, but that, of course, soon becomes a waste of time. Make a habit of modifying trustee rights to user groups and containers and not to individuals.

Security is one of the most important administrative tasks for any network manager. More security processes are discussed later in this part.

Working with properties and objects

The following list describes areas with which you need to concern yourself most of the time as you manage objects and their properties:

✦ **Directory rights:** Apply only to the file system directory and are part of the file system. Directory rights *flow downhill,* in that subdirectories inherit all the rights of their parent directories (just as with human parents and children) unless you specifically block those rights. You may grant to any user object directory rights to any directory.

✦ **File rights:** Apply only to the individual file to which you assign them. Trustee objects inherit rights to files in a directory based on their rights to the directory holding the files.

✦ **Object rights:** Apply only to NDS objects, which inherit them from higher objects. Rights that you assign directly to an object do not pass down the line with continued inheritance.

✦ **Property rights:** Apply only to the properties of NDS objects and don't influence the object itself — just the access rights to that object. Property rights that you assign aren't inheritable either.

✦ **All Property rights:** Apply to all rights of any given object, which you assign all at once by selecting one check box. These rights are inheritable and flow down the NDS tree, unlike the previous two rights in this list.

The intelligent use of inheritance and the understanding that only certain rights are inheritable make your network administration more effective and less time-consuming.

Working with audit facilities

The IRS isn't the only group with a fearsome audit — NetWare has one, although few people utilize the available features. A few third-party products provide some audit capabilities, but none of them focus strictly on auditing, as does the AUDITCON utility.

AUDIT CONfiguration is another DOS utility, built with the C-Worthy interface, so you need to run it from the DOS command line.

Serious auditing and network management call for an optional product. Several are available, but ManageWise from Novell is by far the best for any network — and especially for a NetWare network. ManageWise Version 2.6 even adds the capability to monitor more than 130 different NDS actions and error conditions and send alerts to the management console or even to pagers, depending on the severity of the problem. If your network uptime is critical, AUDITCON can't do anywhere near the job of ManageWise, but AUDITCON is free with NetWare.

You do your auditing per server and not through NDS. This requirement is for security purposes, because a distributed audit process spread over the same servers as NDS wouldn't be particularly secure. Only auditable resources for the container that you log in on appear in the AUDITCON menu. The audits are tied to the physical server and volumes, and tracking the security of subsequent audit files is an important consideration. Unsecured audit files are unacceptable and not trusted in most audit situations.

The Auditor can be a separate user from any of the network administrators — if that's important in your company. To start an audit of a volume, follow these steps:

1. Log in as the ADMIN user or equivalent and change context to the container holding the volume to audit.

2. Verify that the Auditor user (who can be any user with Read and File Scan rights to SYS:PUBLIC) has Browse rights in the containers that you want the Auditor to monitor. Using NWADMIN to check the Auditor's rights to files and directories is explained toward the end of this part.

3. Type **AUDITCON** at the DOS command line.

4. Choose Available Audit Options⇨Enable Volume Auditing from the menu bar.

5. If the program asks for one, provide a password for the Auditor user and step out of the loop.

Why does the Auditor have a password? Because the Auditor isn't an administrator and should be completely separate from the network support staff. Having the people in charge of managing the network also do their own auditing doesn't make sense. Do you think that those same people are likely to unearth any serious problems? Every business should use outside auditors to isolate the audit results from any suspicion.

After the initial setup, any Auditor user can carry out his business without talking to the network administrator. If the Auditor changes his account password, the Supervisor can't see any of the Auditor's work files or saved reports, ensuring security.

To audit, follow these steps:

1. Type **AUDITCON** from the DOS command line.

2. Choose Auditing Configuration.

3. Choose to audit by event, by file/directory, or by user.

4. Specify the event, file/directory, or user to focus on for the audit.

5. Verify saving the changes and exit.

The next step is to view these audit reports; again, you have some flexibility in doing so. You can save older audits (through the Auditing Reports menu command) and view them at a later date. Tracking several older audit files helps establish a baseline for network operations that often becomes important. Filters for report outputs include the following options:

+ Date/time

+ Event

+ Exclude paths/files

+ Exclude users

+ Include paths/files

+ Include users

You have more event options for users, files, servers, and printers than you want to worry about until you face a specific problem. Rest assured that you can track some of the most obscure

NetWare events if you really want to. Then you can save the audit files and generate reports over time, compare different times, and see operational changes. But this process can be extremely mind-numbing, unless you're looking for something particular. Anything more detailed than file deletions or inappropriate accesses may get bogged down in the process of auditing. Focus on users suspected of misdeeds to keep your focus narrow.

Protecting login scripts

NetWare 3.*x* ties login scripts to each user, because that's pretty much how the Bindery database works on each server. NetWare 3.*x* has a *system login script* but only one for the entire server.

NetWare 4.*x* and NetWare 5 assign login scripts to the containers in place of the system script in NetWare 3.*x*. You may quickly and easily copy each container login script to serve other containers if necessary.

Protecting the container login scripts is pretty easy, because most users don't have any rights to modify any of the container details. Group login scripts — for groups of users not always in the same container — also are out of reach of the users.

Experienced network managers discourage individual login scripts for the following two reasons:

✦ If you start making individual login scripts, you spend the rest of your life modifying one login script at a time — a terrible waste of time.

✦ Individuals have rights to Read and Write their own login scripts. This situation comes from the early days of NetWare, when Novell expected users to manage themselves.

Making individual login scripts is a bad idea, but if you do so, protect yourself as much as possible, which involves locking users out of managing their own login scripts. This precaution calls for a change of trustee rights, because the default setting is for them to read and write their login scripts.

Here's how to change a trustee right to a user's login script:

1. Open NWADMIN from your management station.

2. Right-click the User object to modify.

3. Click the Rights to Other Objects command from the pop-up menu.

4. Click OK in the Search Context dialog box.

5. Highlight the user, click the Selected Properties radio button, and highlight Login Script in the list.

6. Click the Write box to clear the check mark, which takes away that right.

7. Click OK to save and exit.

Notice all the other Property Rights change. That's why the default for most properties is Read and only a few have Write rights as well.

The fewer things users can change, the fewer things you'll have to fix.

Using the MONITOR utility

Few utilities are as useful or as well named as MONITOR. Run from the server console (or from your workstation using the RCONSOLE command), this utility truly monitors everything about your server. MONITOR is a server-centric utility — even in this age of distributed network services via NDS.

NetWare 3.*x* settled most of the MONITOR details, but NetWare 4.*x* added one real time-saver by putting the SERVMAN utility inside the Available Options menu of MONITOR. A few other details, such as showing how many processors are active, reflect NetWare's growing capabilities to support such things as multiple processor servers. SERVMAN is an advanced server configuration tool outside the scope of this reference.

Get familiar with MONITOR, because it can help you quite a bit. Load the utility at the server console's colon prompt by typing the following line:

```
LOAD MONITOR
```

Take screenshots of your server's status now and then so that you have an easy-to-reference record of normal server operations.

The General Information screen that appears when you start MONITOR gives a quick display of your server's health. The more Total cache buffers you have, the more memory you have available to support users. If your Utilization number on this screen is stuck way up in high numbers, you have an overworked server.

In the Available Options menu, the last option, although displaying the label Server Parameters, is really SERVMAN. The first menu item, Connections, offers a list of all user and software server connections — a handy option that enables you to highlight user names and press the Delete key to clear them off the server if you need everyone off the system for backups and the like.

MONITOR gives you the following six options when loading, depending on which version of NetWare you're using:

✦ **N:** No screensaver snake. (The same option is NS in NetWare 3.*x*.)

✦ **T nn:** Time before screensaver activation. Replace the *nn* with the number of seconds before the screensaver activates. (NetWare 5 has a separate screensaver program.)

✦ **M:** Activates the screensaver only if the MONITOR program is on-screen at the time.

✦ **L:** Locks the MONITOR console, requiring the supervisor password to unlock. Great to place in the AUTOEXEC.NCF file to safely start the MONITOR after the server boots. Check Novell's online documentation for AUTOEXEC.NCF change help.

✦ **P:** Shows processor information (in NetWare 3.*x* only).

✦ **NH:** Loads MONITOR without the Help screens, which saves about 25K of server RAM (in NetWare 3.*x* only).

 NetWare 5 offers the new Java-based ConsoleOne utility, which shows all MONITOR information and more in graphical format. Do nothing; ConsoleOne starts automatically.

Maintaining DNS with DSREPAIR

DSREPAIR isn't often necessary if you're running NetWare 4.*x* and NetWare 5, but it does come in handy eventually. This utility runs from the server console colon prompt and you call it by typing the following line:

```
LOAD DSREPAIR
```

Available Options is the main menu heading, and Unattended full repair is the first, and most often used, menu choice. When you press Enter on Unattended full repair, most minor NDS problems are fixed automatically. That's why Novell calls it the *Unattended* Full-Repair option.

DSREPAIR is another server-centric utility that works on one server's database at a time. Repairs include records, scheme, Bindery objects, and external references. DSREPAIR has only one startup option: *U,* for Unload immediately after running.

The next most popular option is on the Available Options menu — Time Synchronization. NDS is extremely time-sensitive in that servers must agree on a time so they can agree on the correct sequence of time-stamped events. If Unattended Full Repair doesn't fix your NDS problems, try Time Synchronization.

Combining trees by using DSMERGE

NetWare 4.0 didn't allow you to reconfigure trees, which caused some level of consternation among early adopters. Novell wisely added the DSMERGE utility in NetWare 4.11 to merge the roots of two NDS trees and make changing the name of a tree easier. Always backup before making major server changes.

DSMERGE is another server console prompt utility that doesn't have any options. All users must be logged out for this operation; type **DISABLE LOGIN** at the server colon prompt to block anyone trying to sneak onto the network. To start, go to the server console colon prompt and type the following line:

```
LOAD DSMERGE
```

Check Servers in this Tree is the first menu option for this utility and the first option you should choose before you try to mash trees together. Then choose Check Time Synchronization to verify that all the servers are communicating correctly. After you're ready, perform the following steps to merge the two trees:

1. Choose Merge Two Trees on the Available Options menu and press Enter.

2. Provide the ADMIN name and password for the local tree.

3. Choose the target tree from the pick list that appears after you press Enter, and then provide the ADMIN name and password for that tree.

4. Press F10 to begin the merge process.

Give the network plenty of time to settle down, because this operation causes quite a bit of NDS activity, as you can imagine.

Defining user environment settings by using NETUSER and NetWare User Tools

Novell has been providing helpful network navigation tools for users since the beginning of NetWare, but that trend may end soon. NETUSER in NetWare 4.x replaces several other user utilities in NetWare 3.x and has some fun information for users.

As Microsoft Windows 95/98/NT continues to increase its desktop market share past the 90 percent mark, Novell refers users to Microsoft's Network Neighborhood. This referral doesn't bode well, however, for the continued availability of NETUSER or NetWare User Tools.

The DOS program NETUSER is available in the SYS:PUBLIC directory. You start it from the DOS command line by typing the program name with no options. Every user has access, and the username passes to NETUSER automatically, so the program knows who the user is and what access to the network that user has.

NETUSER enables users to perform the following tasks:

✦ See and/or change their context.

✦ See their login name.

✦ View their printer connections.

✦ See whether they can accept SEND messages from other users.

✦ Capture or change printers for up to nine parallel printer ports.

✦ Send messages to users or groups or turn their own message receipt off.

✦ Check or change drive and search-drive mappings.

✦ See attached servers, change their login script, change their password, or view standard NetWare server information.

Pretty useful for a small DOS program, isn't it?

The NetWare User Tools from Novell, designed for Microsoft's Windows 3.1 program to fill in all the missing networking tools Microsoft forgot to include, offers much the same information as NETUSER did but in a prettier format. It doesn't work with Windows 95/98/NT, but Novell's Client32 software does add some of the same functionality inside the Network Neighborhood utility.

Rather than providing menu choices as in NETUSER, NetWare User Tools has a set of icons across the top of the window. Two extra launch buttons support an application name and start-up parameters, making a nice launch platform for some users. The buttons even sport the icons from the chosen applications.

Backing up files with SBACKUP

SBACKUP is another server console utility that loads by typing its name at the server console colon prompt. Now, less a stand-alone utility than part of Novell's Storage Management Services, SBACKUP offers less flexibility and user friendliness than third-party software. However, it comes free with NetWare.

Before backups are possible, you must load a Target Service Agent on either a server or workstation, or both. Loading this small software agent automatically with your other NetWare client files is an option in Client32 software. The NLM version for the server can be put into the AUTOEXEC.BAT file.

To perform a standard, garden-variety server backup session, just follow these steps:

1. Attach an approved tape backup system to the NetWare server.

2. Load the appropriate TSA*xxx* NLM, replacing *xxx* with the server version (410, 400, 312, or 311) by typing **LOAD x** at the server console colon prompt.

3. Type **LOAD SBACKUP** at the server console colon prompt.

4. Choose Backup or Restore, depending on your goal.

5. Identify the target (server) for the session.

6. Choose the volumes, directories, or files to backup or restore.

7. Provide a descriptive name for your backup session.

8. Identify the backup or restore hardware to use.

9. Choose to Append to an existing tape if you want.

10. Press Enter to save your details and start the backup or restore process.

Third-party products often run with the hardware attached to a workstation, enabling some versions to back up multiple servers concurrently. Backup is critical, but restore can be lifesaving, so make sure your system makes quality backups. Backups are easy to restore from, and you can run them unattended during the night.

Better Backup Options

No network administrator function is more critical than protecting files. Backing up files safely, and being able to restore them when necessary, is the job many executives believe absolutely defines the role of a network administrator.

Administrators know that the majority of file restores are necessitated by user mistakes, but don't say so out loud.

So your goal as a backup administrator (many companies regard data safety so important they have a position like this) is to make life as simple for yourself as possible while providing maximum data protection. The better the tool you have for backup and restore, the better off your company. Novell's SBACKUP is better than it was, but it lags far behind several third-party options.

Hardware backup product options

Backup media in the old days were floppy disks. That didn't work well, and no one in their right mind ever made a complete backup to floppies more than once.

Tape systems became the defacto backup standard as soon as they appeared for NetWare. Even a tape that only stored 30MB was better than floppy disks.

Newcomers to the backup field challenge tape systems in a variety of ways: cost, convenience, and reliability. Tape hardware now includes libraries stacking groups of tape together to backup hundreds of gigabytes without operator intervention. These are great devices, but they have high price tags. Tape options today include getting up to ten or more gigabytes on a single tape cartridge, so the tape vendors are constantly improving to keep their market share.

Some other backup hardware options include:

+ **CD-R drives:** Compact Disk-Readable drives provide a backup good literally forever, but the disks can only be written to once. Great for snapshots of accounting data every time a financial milestone, such as quarter closing, is reached.

+ **CD-RW drives:** Compact Disk-Read Writable drives provide the backup quality of CD-ROM and include the capability to rewrite disks. Think of these as stiff tapes, and rotate them accordingly. The problem with these is the low capacity of the CD when compared to tape.

+ **DAT:** Digital Audio Tape format, borrowed from the video world, uses 4mm tape (a pretty small little cartridge) with the capability, depending on compression ratios, to store up to 12GB on a single tape cartridge.

+ **8mm tape:** Precursor to 4mm DAT drives, developed by the Exabyte Corporation and licensed by other hardware vendors, capable of storing up to 20GB per tape.

+ **DLT:** Digital Linear Tape, a high-end technology using half-inch tape to cram up to 35GB of data onto a single tape cartridge.

Ten backup commandments

You should follow these ten backup commandments:

1. Back up data every day your company is open.

2. Rotate backup tapes intelligently.

3. Store your rotation tapes offsite.

4. Check backup quality by restoring test files from random tapes weekly.

5. Follow your tape hardware manufacturer's cleaning schedule.

6. Replace tapes following the tape manufacturer's replacement schedule.

7. Back up your entire server so complete replacements will be much more convenient.

8. Remember the "backup" user has complete rights to your network, so monitor that security hole.

9. Keep on-site tapes in a fireproof, waterproof location.

10. Keep hard copies of critical accounting, sales, and product files.

EXTRA: Paranoia pays in the backup business.

One proven tape rotation plan

Commandment number two says to rotate back up tapes intelligently. Vague instructions often lead to surprises, and surprises are best avoided in network management.

Because some of you may not have a tape rotation plan you're happy with, take a look at the following. You don't have to follow this if you don't want to, but at least it's a start.

First, the requirements:

✦ 20 tapes for daily use

✦ 6 tapes for weekly use

✦ 13 tapes for yearly use

✦ 1 extra tape

Budget-minded readers may quickly shriek that all adds up to 40 tapes, and tapes can be expensive. Yes, tapes can be expensive. But no tape costs more than the time needed to re-create a critical file.

Follow this rotation schedule:

✦ Every week, the oldest tape moves from Daily to Weekly use.

✦ Every month, the oldest tape moves from Weekly to Monthly use.

✦ Every month, the oldest tape moves from Monthly to Daily use.

Will this system work for you? Try it and find out, or use this as a starting point to develop your own rotation plan.

Why 13 tapes for monthly use, and 6 for weekly use? Because accounting periods, sales periods, and projects tend to end on the week, month, quarter, or year. What good are ten yearly tapes, if you discover you need last year's reconciliation report, and that tape is now holding the data from last Thursday? Not much, so make sure you have a year plus a month to cover your assets as well as possible.

A sample third-party backup system

Novell doesn't make backup hardware, so in one sense all NetWare backup systems are third party. We don't want to make an endorsement of any particular third-party hardware and software combination, but an examination of one such system will help you see what is important when considering a backup system of your own.

Our example is Legato Networker, from Legato Systems, Inc., (www.legato.com). Why Legato? They were the first to back up both Unix and NetWare systems to a single tape (as far as we know), and that technical foresight bodes well for their continued success. Besides that, many networks today have a mix of NetWare, Windows NT, and Unix systems. A single tape backup system to cover all those bases may be very welcome in your company.

Legato is one of just a handful of options: One popular trade magazine's Web site provided 42 options in a table of enterprise backup software. Each of the 42 systems is able to backup one or all of the Big Three Network Operating Systems of NetWare, Windows NT, and Unix. But Legato was the first we got our hands on, years ago, and that fondness for the first in the market causes us to list Legato as an example.

The following bullet points, indicative of a quality tape backup system, are strongly influenced by the Legato product:

✦ Complies with Novell's Storage Management Server (SMS) specifications

✦ Backs up all NetWare server information

✦ Provides an index to find backed-up files quickly

✦ Includes strong tape checking and verification software

✦ Allows you to back up from a workstation or a NetWare server-attached tape device

✦ Offers disaster recovery help to rebuild entire server data-sets quickly

✦ Includes a graphical management program, including drag and drop

✦ Offers a consistent look to all NetWare platform backups, even with different NetWare software versions in the mix

✦ Is fully automated option for late-night backup

✦ Strong data compression is mandatory, the capability to back up multiple clients at once is a wonderful bonus

✦ Scales up to support a growing network's backup needs

✦ Is easy to add new clients, servers, and volumes

✦ Configures software to take advantage of faster hardware

✦ Keeps throughput relatively constant as more backup server targets are added

✦ Offers a way to back up client stations as well as NetWare servers

✦ Supports a wide variety of tape drives and autochangers

Notice the last point. High-end systems, such as Legato, offer at some levels just the software to turbo-charge your existing hardware by adding new capabilities.

You may buy your hardware from one dealer and then buy replacement software from another dealer. Companies that specialize in hardware development often make deals with software developers to include software, but that software is never the highest-quality software the developers have available.

Remote backup options

In this case, remote does mean from your office in the basement to the servers on the third floor. Several companies specialize in accepting backup data across the Internet or a private network connection.

Does this work? Is this safe? Yes and yes. It works better with fast network connections, and compression and encryption ensure the safety across the network. Believe it or not, this technology has been around since the 1960s and early mainframe off-site service bureaus.

Common features to look for when discussing "televaulting" services:

✦ Transmission and storage compression

✦ Capability to upload only changes to file sets

✦ Encryption during transmission and storage

✦ 24-hour availability

✦ Virus filtering during upload

✦ Option to provide a backup copy to you on CD-ROM

NetWare Server Installation

You may think that you install a NetWare server only once, but our experience is that servers often take multiple installations, and every network adds servers, meaning more installations are necessary. Besides, by the time that you get a server completely installed, your network plans may have changed, making it easier to reinstall your server than try to rework everything.

The totally quick CD-ROM install

We're going to assume that this installation is of the first, second, or even third NetWare server for your network. If you don't have any custom configuration details for your server and volumes, the installation process is much more straightforward than is that of installing a desktop operating system today. Just follow these steps:

1. Put the NetWare CD into the CD-ROM drive.

   See Part II for system requirements and server preparation.

2. Type **INSTALL** at the CD-ROM drive prompt.

3. Accept the defaults.

4. Provide a unique name for your server.

5. Reboot your server.

This process may look truncated, but it's exactly what you do on your second or third server installation.

Building a registration disk

The more information that Novell's technical support department has about your network, the more they can help you. That's why Novell introduced the Registration Diskette with NetWare 4.0 instead of trusting you to send back scrawled information on a postcard. Follow these yellow bricks down the road:

1. Type **LOAD INSTALL** (**NWCONFIG** for NetWare 5) at the server console colon prompt.

2. Highlight Product Options and press Enter.

3. Choose Create Registration Diskette.

4. Press F10 after the legalese notice screen.

5. Provide details about your reseller and press F10.

6. Provide information about your company and network, and press F10.

7. Accept the offer to include server-specific information.

8. Mail the diskette in the provided mailer.

Better than putting a postcard on your desk and losing it, isn't it?

Creating client installation disks

New clients without CD-ROM drives need installation diskettes. Sorry — you should have sprung for the CD-ROM drive so that you could use the NetWare Client CD-ROM and install these new stations much more quickly. Here are the extra steps that you must perform to make up for that lack of foresight:

1. Type **LOAD INSTALL** (or **NWCONFIG** for NetWare 5) at the server console colon prompt.

2. Choose Product Options.

3. Choose Create DOS/MS Windows/OS2 Client Install Diskettes.

4. Choose the type of installation diskettes you want.

5. Insert blank, formatted diskettes of the type that the program requests as often as you need to.

6. Label the diskettes as suggested by the routine.

If you don't label the diskettes, you're sure to drop them before you reach the first machine. The disk label that you see in checking the disk contents tells you which disk is which.

Installing a new language

After NetWare 4.01 became multilingual, it offered better support for multiple languages and non-English NetWare servers with each upgrade. To install a new language, perform the following steps:

1. Type **LOAD INSTALL** (or **NWCONFIG** for NetWare 5) at the server console colon prompt.

2. Choose Product Options.

3. Choose Install an Additional Server Language.

4. Specify the source of the language files.

5. Choose the language-specific files to install.

Follow the directions, and all turns out fine. The only tricky part is finding this operation, adding server languages, buried along with new products in the INSTALL or NWCONFIG programs.

Changing language choice

After you install the new language files, you probably want to use them. Just follow these steps:

1. Type **LOAD INSTALL** (or **NWCONFIG** for NetWare 5) at the server console colon prompt.

2. Choose Product Options.

3. Choose Change Server Language.

4. Specify the server language files source.

5. Select the default server language.

6. Clear all users and server connections.

7. Reboot the server.

Because you need to present the information files in the new default language, you must reboot to enable the server to read all the correct language files from the beginning.

Installing online docs

Handy documentation is a blessing. NetWare enables you to load the entire electronic manual set onto the server for easy access; just follow these steps:

1. Type **LOAD INSTALL** at the server console colon prompt.

2. Choose Product Options.

3. Choose Install Online Documentation and Viewers.

4. Verify the location of the documentation files.

5. Choose the file sets that you want to install.

6. Specify the destination of the documentation files.

NetWare 5 beta software changes the rules on this process a little, and they're likely to stay changed. The Documentation CD-ROM disk has an installation program in the root directory. Load this CD into a workstation drive and choose to install documentation and you may put the files on your local machine or on the server. The reader is changing from a proprietary reader to a Web browser, so more of your users can read the documentation with the software they already have on their computers.

Removing NDS

Don't remove NDS if you have a choice, or there's any hope of reworking NDS on your network. Really. If you must take your network's life in your hands, just follow these steps:

1. Type **LOAD INSTALL** (or **NWCONFIG** for NetWare 5) at the server console colon prompt.

2. Choose Directory Options.

3. Choose Remove Directory Services from this server.

4. Read the NDS warnings.

5. Acknowledge that you still want to delete NDS from this server.

6. Log in as Admin or equivalent.

7. Read more NDS warnings and reconsider.

8. Verify your intention to blow away NDS.

9. Read more warnings and then press Enter.

This procedure is not for the faint of heart. The operation is server-centric, so if you're going to replace or delete NDS on multiple servers, you must follow this operation for each server. Follow the installation instructions at the beginning of this reference to install NDS once again.

Printing Tasks

People don't trust computers, and many don't believe that information is real until it comes out of the computer and they can hold the paper in their hands and actually read the information. These people may waste a lot of paper, but some of them may also be your bosses, so printing remains a critical network function.

NetWare is getting much better about printing support. Those tactile folks, itching for paper, don't bother you as much as before, because the printers seem to work better with each NetWare upgrade.

Another casualty of DOS command line management utilities is PCONSOLE. Through NetWare 4.11, PCONSOLE kept up with NWADMIN menu for menu, function for function. NetWare 5's Beta 3 software, the latest we have as this book goes to press, doesn't include PCONSOLE. There's always a chance PCONSOLE will be added, or that an earlier version of PCONSOLE will work with NetWare 5, but the handwriting's on the wall. And it reads: "Go graphical, young manager, go graphical." So we plan to do so.

All the printing functions that we list in this section you can perform in PCONSOLE (through NetWare 4.11). If you have a version earlier than NetWare 5, you can still use PCONSOLE if you want. Take the menu choices that we show you here, and you can follow along in PCONSOLE without trouble.

All the following operations assume that you have NWADMIN loaded for your particular workstation and ready to go.

Using NWADMIN Quick Setup

Quick Setup means exactly what it says: You add a first, or additional, printer quickly by using all the defaults; just follow these steps:

1. Highlight the container that's to host the new printer functions.

2. Open the Tools menu and choose Print Service Quick Setup.

3. Accept all the defaults for printer, print queue, and print server names.

4. If the printer is attached to the file server, click the Communication button to specify that the Connection Type is Auto Load, because it's local to the Print Server.

5. Click the Create button.

Go load your printer with paper and tell your users that the new printer is ready.

Creating a print server object

A print server may be the NetWare software running on the server, a remote print server running from a NetWare client, or another system with enough intelligence somewhere else on the network. To create a print server object, complete the following steps:

1. Right-click the container to hold the new print server.

2. Choose the Create menu option from the pop-up menu.

3. Fill in the Print Server name field in the Create Print Server dialog box.

4. If necessary, check to define additional properties or to create another print queue.

5. Click the Create button.

You need only one print server to support many print queues and printers.

Creating a print queue object

Print queues are really what NetWare users send their print jobs to; we just tell them it's the printer. The print queue holds print jobs until the printer is ready for the job. Creating a new print queue is simple — just follow these steps:

1. Right-click the container to hold the new print queue.

2. Choose the Create menu option in the pop-up menu.

3. Double-click Print Queue to open the Create Print Queue dialog box.

4. Fill in the Print Queue name and Print Queue Volume fields.

5. If necessary, check to define additional properties or to create another print queue.

6. Click the Create button.

You need a print queue before you can create a printer to service that queue.

Creating a printer object

You should have only one printer per print queue, unless two identical printers are load-sharing the print queue jobs. To create a printer object, complete the following steps:

1. Right-click the container to hold the new printer.

2. Click Create.

3. Double-click Printer in the New Object dialog box.

4. Provide a name for the printer. Check the box to define additional properties, or to create another printer immediately.

5. Click the Create button.

See why the Quick Printer Setup is so handy?

Viewing print queue assignments

Printers don't work until the print server, print queue, and printer all know about each other and understand the relationship. Your mission is to introduce these three elements and so open the floodgates for print-happy users. To view print queue assignments, complete the following steps:

1. Right-click the print queue you want to check, and then choose Details.

2. Click the Assignments button.

3. Take a look to make sure that the expected print servers and print queue show up in the Assignments display windows.

Don't show up correctly, do they, with lines from server to queue to printer? You need to introduce the new printer to the print server. (See the following section.)

Connect printers to print servers

To connect printers to print servers, perform the following steps:

1. Right-click the print server to support the new printer, and then choose Details.

2. Click the Assignments button.

3. Check the window that lists the printers to see which printers are already configured; to add a new printer, click the Add button.

4. Pick the new printer to add to the print server from the Select Object dialog box and then click OK.

5. Click OK in the Print Server dialog box.

Now all the printers should communicate. To make sure, you need to check one more thing (print layout), as the following section describes.

Viewing print layouts

To view print layouts, perform the following steps:

1. Right-click the print server to support the new printer and then choose Details.

2. Click the Print Layout button.

3. Verify that the lines connecting print server to printer to print queue are all in place. Click the Update button to ensure the latest NDS changes are reflected.

Now's a good time to quickly check that all the printers understand where all their partners in the print process are, shown by linking lines. If a printer has lost its connection to a print server or queue, you're going to have no print joy.

Managing print queues

If you haven't had a user come running and begging you to pull the plug on some runaway print process, you haven't been doing this long enough. Or you're better at hiding than most network administrators.

The Print Queue screen isn't a bad one to check occasionally, even without a user begging you to kill the 400-page report he accidentally routed to the color laser printer. If you don't know how busy your printers are, how can you know when to add another one to the budget? To check out this screen, complete the following steps:

1. Right-click the print queue and then choose Details from the pop-up menu that appears.

2. Click the Job List button.

3. If necessary, right-click any problem print job and click the Delete button.

4. If you prefer, you may hold the print job or get more detailed information by clicking the appropriate command buttons.

User and Group Management

No confusion exists concerning user and group management and whether these functions are best done in the graphical NWADMIN or NETADMIN, the DOS utility. Novell engineers have been pushing us since the beginning of NetWare 4.0 to use NWADMIN for all user and group management.

The good thing about object-oriented management — when you understand how to handle one object, you have a big head start on handling them all.

Some of these management tasks that apply to individual users you may address in the Profile setting. No sense doing the same thing over and over for every user if you can provide a network access foundation for each new user. (For more about profiles, see Part IV.)

Creating user objects

User objects is just a fancy, object-oriented name for *users*. Don't *tell* the users that you treat them as objects — but that's exactly how you should treat them. To create user objects, open NWADMIN from the appropriate workstation and follow these steps:

1. Right-click the container to hold the user, and then click Create in the pop-up menu.

2. Double-click User.

3. Type the user's login name in the login name field.

4. Provide the user's last name.

5. Click the Use An Existing Template check box and then click the Browse button to open the Select Object browsing window if necessary.

6. Click the check boxes Define Additional Properties or Create Another User if necessary.

7. Click the Create button.

The only two pieces of information you must have for users are the login name and the last name. The rest is handy for searching and identification.

Creating user home directories

Creating home directories is easiest if you're creating a new user. Remember the Create Home Directory check box in the previous function? That was the easiest place to create a home directory for a new user.

If you change your mind about giving users home directories, all is not lost. Adding home directories later is not all that much trouble; just follow these steps to create a home directory after the user is created:

1. Open NWADMIN from the appropriate workstation.

2. Right-click the name of the user needing a home directory, and then choose Details.

3. Click the Environment button.

4. Fill out the Volume and Path fields, just below the Home Directory label. If you want to use the Select Object browsing window to find the right place for the home directory, the button for same is to the right of the Volume and Path (still empty) text fields.

5. Provide the volume for the home directory.

6. Provide the path for the home directory within that volume.

7. Click OK to create the home directory.

Behind the scenes, you're granting the users extensive rights to their home directories. Grouping lots of home directories in one volume under an umbrella directory heading, such as Users, makes backups and management all that much easier because you can back up all user data in one directory tree.

Creating group objects

Always look for ways to group users for easier management and security. The group concept has changed little between NetWare 3.x and NetWare 5. To create group objects, open NWADMIN from the appropriate workstation and complete the following steps:

1. Right-click the container to hold the new group, and then choose Details.

2. Double-click Group.

3. Provide a group name and click the check boxes Define Additional Properties and/or Create Another Group, if appropriate.

4. Click the Create button.

A group with no users isn't much good. To add existing users to a new group, follow these steps:

1. Right-click the group that you want to modify and then choose Details from the pop-up menu that appears.

2. Click the Members button.

3. Click the Add button.

4. Pick the users for group membership from the Select Object dialog box by moving up and down the tree as necessary.

5. Click OK.

The other way around this process is to add new users to existing groups. Follow just about the same procedure, except that the button to click in the User dialog box is Group Membership, and then click the Members button. To add the group memberships, follow the same steps as you do to add users to groups, and start by clicking the Add button.

Creating print job configurations

In place of the system print job configuration that was available in NetWare 3.*x*, NetWare 4.*x* and NetWare 5 offer print job configurations tied to containers. This gives more options because different departments can each have default print-job configurations that differ from each other.

Yes, users can each have individual print-job configurations that override parts of their container print-job configuration. But this takes more time than you really want to spend, believe us. Stick with container print-job configurations if at all possible and avoid changing individuals' print job configurations. To create print-job configurations, open NWADMIN from the appropriate workstation and perform the following steps:

1. Right-click the container in which you want to hold the new print-job configurations and then choose Details from the pop-up menu that appears.

2. Click the Print Job Configuration button.

3. Click the New button.

4. Provide a unique Print Job name and other print details in the appropriate fields and then click OK.

Command-line parameters override these configurations. Don't tell anyone but power users about this, or the print-challenged are going to be trashing their print configurations at least twice a week asking you to work some printer magic.

Create/manage user login scripts

Login scripts add much of the flexibility NetWare provides that makes each user feel the network is tailored exactly for them. We suggest that you build login scripts for containers, not individual users, but the process is the same for both.

Container scripts execute first and then user scripts. The last script to run wins any conflicts between settings. To create and manage login script, open NWADMIN from the appropriate workstation and follow these steps:

1. Right-click the object needing a new or modified login script and then choose Details from the pop-up menu that appears.

2. Click the Login Script button.

3. Enter login scripts commands in the large text window filling most of the dialog box.

The User dialog box includes a Profile listing with a Browse button so you can use existing profiles.

4. Click OK to save the login script.

5. Repeat Steps 1 through 4 until you work the kinks out of the login script.

Making too many individual login scripts sucks up much of your time during network setup and reconfigurations — just a word of warning.

Setting user login restrictions

Unlike most options, this function works only on individual users. To set user login restrictions on account expiration, concurrent connections, and ever to disable the account, open NWADMIN from the appropriate workstation and complete the following steps:

1. Right-click the object name of the user needing restrictions and then choose Details from the pop-up menu that appears.

2. Check the appropriate boxes to disable the account, set the account expiration date, or limit the number of concurrent connections.

3. Click OK to save the changes.

Setting login time restrictions

Setting login time restrictions is similar to setting user login restrictions; you also apply login time restrictions only to individual users. Keeping users off the system during backup sessions is the most common use of this feature. To set login time restrictions, open NWADMIN from the appropriate workstation and complete the following steps:

1. Right-click the name of the user needing restrictions, and then choose Details from the pop-up menu that appears.

2. Click the Login Time Restrictions button.

3. To set the restriction, put the mouse pointer on the start time and then press and hold the left mouse button as you drag the dark rectangle across the times during which you want to block the user out of the network.

4. Repeat Step 3 to make as many restriction blocks as you want.

These restricted-time blocks don't need to cover contiguous times.

5. Click OK to save the restrictions.

Setting password restrictions

This restriction is another individual setting, although passwords are generally a matter of policy. This procedure, if nothing else, is an excellent candidate for inclusion in the Profile template. To set or modify password restrictions, open NWADMIN from the appropriate workstation and complete the following steps:

1. Right-click the name of the user you want to restrict and then choose Details from the pop-up menu.

2. Click the Password Restrictions button.

3. Click the check boxes to set the user's password restrictions.

You can set all or none of the check boxes; these settings are mutually exclusive, but all add security. The check boxes are:

• Allow user to change password.

• Require a password (then a text box to use setting for minimum password length).

• Force periodic password changes (then a text box to use setting the number of days between changes). If you prefer, you may use the date and time fields under the "Date password expires" heading to set the next password change time.

- Require unique passwords (the system tracks the last ten passwords and won't allow a repeated password).

- Limit grace logins (how many times the user can skip changing passwords before the system blocks them completely).

4. Click OK to save your settings.

Managing security equivalence

This is a good setting to leave for individuals. Making too many people at one time equivalent in security levels leads to security mistakes. Memories lapse over time, leaving the security holes you created that don't appear anywhere else inside NWADMIN displays. Don't make a habit of this. To manage security equivalence, open NWADMIN from the appropriate workstation and complete the following steps:

1. Right-click the user object that you want to modify and then choose Details from the pop-up window.

2. Click the Security Equal To button.

3. Click the Add button to open the Select Object dialog box so you can browse the tree and find the object that has the security clearance your new object should be equal to.

One user may be equivalent to several other objects. Groups show up for equivalence because you can grant them rights to files and directories.

4. Click OK to save your settings.

Viewing user rights

Often, if a user reports a problem with some network resource, you need to ensure that he has enough assigned rights to do his job. To view user rights, open NWADMIN from the appropriate workstation and complete the following steps:

1. Right-click the object to be checked, and then choose Rights to Other Objects.

2. Verify the context to search for rights, and check the Search Entire Tree check box if necessary.

3. Click OK to start the rights search.

The larger the network, the longer this search process takes. You will need to check the Search Entire Subtree box to find all the objects.

4. Highlight any of the items that appear in the list in the Assigned Objects window after the search.

5. Read the Object rights and Property rights of the individual for the highlighted object.

6. Modify rights as necessary.

7. Click OK to save and exit.

Changing rights to files and directories

You can change rights for containers, user groups, and individuals. To change rights to files and directories, open NWADMIN from the appropriate workstation and complete the following steps:

1. Right-click the object that you want to modify and then choose Details from the pop-up menu that appears.

2. Click the Rights to Files and Directories button.

3. Click the Find button to open the Search Context window so you can find the volume(s) to change access rights.

4. Click the Add button in the Files and Directories section to open the Select Object dialog box.

5. Pick one or more volumes, directories, or files to change the rights of access.

6. Highlight one File or Directories entry and modify the Rights in the bottom of the dialog by checking or unchecking the check boxes.

7. Click OK to save your modifications.

Establishing user account balance

Companies that like to charge departments for network use need some way to track these charges, and NetWare was the first LAN to offer some help. This function is server-centric because each server must turn on Accounting before you can figure the account balance. To establish user account balance, open NWADMIN from the appropriate workstation and complete the following steps:

1. Right-click the user object that needs a balance, and then choose Details.

2. Click the Account Balance button.

3. Provide a number in the Account balance field between minus (–) 99,999,999 and 999,999,999.

This number is compared to the rates you charge for network services and disk space.

4. Click the Allow Unlimited Credit only if you want this user exempt from account-balance restrictions.

5. When unchecked, the Allow Unlimited Credit box allows the Low balance limit to become active. When the user's account balance reaches this limit, the user receives warnings from the system.

6. Click OK to save and exit.

Setting accounting limits makes lots of extra work for you and any other network administrators. If you're the only administrator for your network, consider yourself warned!

Setting volume space restrictions

More useful than accounting is saving some disk space from greedy users. This utility keeps disk hogs from taking over your network disk space. To set volume space restrictions, open NWADMIN from the appropriate workstation and complete the following steps:

1. Right-click the volume needing restrictions added, and then choose Details.

2. Click the User Space Limits button.

3. Click the Search Context browser button to list users needing restrictions.

4. Highlight the user needing restrictions and then click the Modify button.

5. Click the Limited Volume Space check box in the Volume Space Restriction area.

6. Set the amount of disk space, in Ks, you're allocating to this user.

7. Click OK.

8. Highlight any other users needing restrictions and repeat Steps 3 through 7 as needed.

Disks are cheap today, but that doesn't mean that some limits are out of place. You can undo this restriction easily if disk space becomes plentiful again and then apply it again to help "encourage" users to clean out the junk from their server directories.

Setting intruder detection

Security is a concern of all networks. Setting intruder detection for a container can help trap outsiders trying to sneak onto your network — or, more likely, insiders trying to guess a coworker's password. To turn on intruder detection, open NWADMIN from the appropriate workstation and complete the following steps:

1. Right-click the container requiring intruder detection and choose Details from the pop-up menu.

2. Click the Intruder Detection button.

3. Click the Detect intruders check box.

4. Type the number of incorrect login attempts you're willing to allow in the text box.

5. Set the days, hours, and minutes to reset the detection counter for that workstation.

6. If you prefer, click the Lock Account after Detection check box.

   Set the days, hours, and minutes to keep that workstation locked from any login attempts.

7. Click OK to save and exit.

Do you want to severely punish someone trying to guess a coworker's password? Of course you do. But that's a management decision. Your job is only to set the trap if someone is attempting to hack your network.

Resetting intruder lockout

Regular, trustworthy employees who forget their passwords cause most lockouts. If they come to you to resolve their lockout problems, they may be apologetic, contrite, confused, hostile, or all four at once.

Resetting a locked account is simple:

1. Right-click the username, and then choose Details.

2. Click the Intruder Lockout button.

3. Clear the Account Locked check box.

4. Click OK to save the changes.

Part VII

Making the NetWare-to-Internet Connection

Novell has made a lot of noise recently about how Internet-friendly NetWare has become, and that's actually the truth. Novell servers can now participate fully as Internet Web servers and Internet gateways, and they even add extra security to protect your existing network against Internet interlopers.

Do these changes mean that you have to buy a new NetWare 5 server to take advantage of all this Internet interaction? Not at all. NetWare 4.*x* does a good job of adding the Internet to your local network, although the pieces aren't packaged as neatly as they are with NetWare 5. Even NetWare 3.*x* networks can join in the Internet fun.

In this part . . .

- ✔ **Understanding why NetWare includes TCP/IP**

- ✔ **Configuring network settings and protocols with INETCFG**

Adding TCP/IP to NetWare

Novell engineers and executives fought the brave fight against TCP/IP, but they lost. Much to their credit, they have now stopped fighting against TCP/IP and they've worked to make NetWare the best TCP/IP-driven network server and operating system on the market today.

The conversion to TCP/IP has not been easy, and it's been a continuous process since NetWare 3.11. Well, *conversion* is not the right word, because IPX/SPX is fully supported on NetWare 5. Novell executives have loudly proclaimed that Novell will support IPX/SPX for the next 100 years.

Comparing IPX/SPX and TCP/IP

First, some similarities between IPX/SPX and TCP/IP:

+ IPX and TCP/IP are resident in both the server and client machines.

+ Both need unique network identification numbers for every system on the network.

+ Both send multiple packets at once while awaiting a single confirmation, speeding up performance.

+ Both client software sets are easy to find for free. (NetWare includes IPX and TCP/IP; Windows 95/98/NT includes TCP/IP and IPX in their NetWare client software.)

+ Both have a variety of diagnostic tools and management software available.

Now, for some advantages of IPX over TCP/IP:

+ Takes less RAM

+ Runs faster

+ More software written for IPX than any other network protocol

+ Automatically configures all network addressing

Now, for the main advantage of TCP/IP over IPX:

+ It runs the Internet.

You probably noticed that we only listed one advantage of TCP/IP over IPX. This is a short list, and like the proverbial trump card, it ends the discussion. Yeah, IPX offers more advantages for networking than TCP/IP, but the world has spoken.

New network transport protocol options

Because of the advantage of running on the Internet, TCP/IP has won the war, and IPX will become another niche protocol in about 20 years. What does this mean to you as a network manager?

Not much extra work, because NetWare handles most of the TCP/IP setup automatically. Client-to-server communications over TCP/IP have been possible since NetWare 4.1. You can find out how to make your NetWare network communicate over TCP/IP later in this part.

The big difference between NetWare 5 and previous versions is TCP/IP's status as the default network transport protocol for NetWare. Before, IPX was the default, and TCP/IP required some work to be put into operation. Now, TCP/IP is the default, but thankfully it's easier to install. NetWare 5 servers can support IPX and TCP/IP concurrently, and all TCP/IP networks can run some gateway software in the server to connect all TCP/IP clients on one network to more-traditional IPX network resources on another network.

Configuring Network Settings and Protocols with INETCFG

INETCFG (InterNETworking ConFiGuration) handles the grunt work of adding or modifying protocol support for NetWare servers. This utility is server-centric because it controls the boards in a single server. This utility runs from the server console colon prompt.

Many network administration chores require INETCFG because protocol management has become an important part of local area networks. As Novell changes from IPX to TCP/IP for its standard client-to-server network-transport protocol, administrators can expect to spend lots of time inside INETCFG.

Here's a quick tour of what you see in INETCFG after you type **LOAD INETCFG** at the server console colon prompt and see the menu titled Internetworking Configuration:

+ **Boards:** Add a new network board (another name for network interface card) or modify the hardware parameters of an existing board.

+ **Network Interfaces:** Only used for WAN boards; used to configure individual board details.

+ **WAN Call Directory:** Sets the numbers, dialing details, and connection options for WAN boards linking the server to others or to dial-up networks.

✦ **Protocols:** Allows you to enable and configure network protocols, including AppleTalk, IPX, Source Route Bridge, Source Route End Station (both options used for token ring networks), TCP/IP, and User-Specified Protocol.

✦ **Bindings:** Enables you to connect protocol settings to a previously specified network interface.

✦ **Manage Configuration:** Handles configurations as a group, like making copies of configuration files and loading configurations from a diskette.

✦ **View Configuration:** Gives you the read-only option to view — but not change — all board, protocol, and configuration files.

✦ **Reinitialize System:** Flushes current settings from the server and reloads settings based on current parameters within INETCFG.

INETCFG controls five files:

✦ AURP.CFG

✦ TCPIP.CFG

✦ IPXSPX.CFG

✦ NLSP.CFG

✦ NETINFO.CFG

Do not edit these files or handle them in any way. If you make any changes or move these files, INETCFG will be lost or your network may quit.

IP address cheat sheet

The biggest handicap NetWare administrators face is IP addressing. One of the best traits of NetWare addressing is that you simply don't do any. NetWare takes the address of the interface card and hooks it to the address of the network segment defined at the server, and addressing is finished.

TCP/IP addressing, or IP addressing when you're talking officially about the networking communications part of TCP/IP, requires much more work, which is why NetWare administrators believe the subject is so difficult and despair over getting it right. Tons of books are available on this subject, showing that TCP/IP administrators don't understand this addressing either and that they also despair over getting it right. Misery does love company.

An IP address is four bytes long, and it is listed as four numbers with periods in between: xxx.xxx.xxx.xxx. Each xxx can be a number between 0 and 255. The top number is 255 because that's as high as a single byte can go.

Each byte is either a network or host designator. To keep track, the first number is divided into three sections for Class A, B, and C addresses. We show this using numbers and *h*s for host addresses and *n*s for network addresses.

+ Class A addresses range from 1.h.h.h to 127.h.h.h (0 and 128 are reserved numbers). Only 126 Class A addresses are available; all are long gone.

+ Class B addresses range from 129.h.n.n to 191.h.n.n. The h part in the second range goes from 1 to 254, leaving some reserved addresses again. More than 16,000 Class B addresses are available. These are also long gone.

+ Class C addresses range from 192.h.h.n to 223.h.h.n. The h part in the second and third ranges goes from 1 to 254, making a total of more than 16 million Class C addresses. Those are available, but are too expensive for small companies to justify.

There are other addressing classes that use some new math-type tricks. A good reference for these are white papers at Novell, Microsoft, and other network equipment vendors. You can find some if you do a search on "TCP/IP white paper" on the Internet.

If your company has some Unix Web servers around, someone understands (at least minimally) TCP/IP addressing. When you get ready to connect your NetWare server to the TCP/IP network, go to that person and make sure you follow all numbering and addressing instructions exactly. Any typos or mistakes can really clobber your network.

Configuring and using TCP/IP

NetWare 3.*x* and 4.*x* add TCP/IP support, but not as the default choice. TCP/IP support means going into INETCFG during or after installation and returning now and then to make changes. If you're connected to the Internet, it also means making sure that an appropriate IP addressing scheme is in use, so that your users can access Internet resources and possibly, so that other users on the Internet can access your resources. With NetWare 5, on the other hand, TCP/IP is very much a part of the basic NetWare picture. Given the ubiquity of Internet access and use, therefore, you should dig into the topics and services that TCP/IP can provide in a NetWare environment.

To learn more about TCP/IP in the NetWare environment, consult the online documentation for NetWare using *TCP/IP* as your search term. You can also obtain more information by using the same approach on the Novell Web site at www.novell.com.

Now that we've warned you beforehand, here's how to activate
TCP/IP on a NetWare server — just follow these steps:

1. Type **LOAD INETCFG** from the server console colon prompt.

2. Choose Protocols, and then TCP/IP from the Protocol Configuration menu.

3. Press Escape and say Yes to accept the default settings (TCP/IP
enabled as an end node. Change IP Packet Forwarding to
"Enabled" for routing functions).

4. Press Escape and then choose Bindings from the main menu.

5. Choose the protocol-to-interface binding to support TCP/IP
and press Enter.

6. Press Enter on TCP/IP and then press Enter again.

7. Provide the server's TCP/IP address and subnet mask. Ask
your Internet network expert if you don't know these numbers.

8. Press Escape to save recent changes and press Escape again
to save all the changes.

9. Reboot the server to activate the new protocol.

After saving the TCP/IP configuration, your server separates
normal server information from the AUTOEXEC.NCF file into other
specialized protocol files. You should make changes only through
INETCFG or the files could become corrupted.

Installing an IPX/IP Gateway

Just because the server can use TCP/IP to communicate doesn't
mean that the clients can do the same. Clients must either add the
TCP/IP protocol on their own if they want to communicate with
the Internet and World Wide Web directly or use a gateway.

DOS and Windows 3.1 systems must pay for TCP/IP support, and
the cost ranges from free to hundreds of dollars per computer,
depending on the TCP/IP package. Although Windows 95/98/NT
software includes a minimum set of TCP/IP protocol software,
many companies prefer to keep TCP/IP off their workstations for
address management and security reasons. So you're back to the
need for a gateway to reach the Internet or World Wide Web.

Novell added the IPX/IP Gateway to NetWare starting with
IntranetWare, but it is also included with BorderManager. The
gateway relies on a simple trick to work its magic: All traffic
between clients and the gateway use IPX, and the gateway converts IPX to TCP/IP to make connections outside the local network. On the return trip (from the outside world to the local
network), the protocol swap reverses from TCP/IP to IPX, and the

gateway keeps track of client activity and routes incoming packets to the appropriate recipients automatically.

Gateway software must reside on each client and at least one NetWare server. Installing the software on the clients is simple: Check the IPX/IP Gateway box during Client32 setup or run the SETUP program that's on the server. To install IPX/IP Gateway on the server via the SETUP program, follow these steps:

1. Verify that the host server for the IPX/IP Gateway has TCP/IP support correctly installed and is active.

2. Put the Internet Access Server 4 CD-ROM in the server's CD-ROM drive.

3. Type **LOAD INSTALL** (or **LOAD NWCONFIG** for NetWare 5) on the server console at the colon prompt.

4. Choose Product Options⇨Install a Product Not Listed.

5. Answer No after the program queries you about installing configuration files to the server.

6. Inside INETCFG, choose Protocols⇨TCP/IP and then choose the IPX/IP Gateway Configuration choice at the bottom of the screen.

7. Enable the IPX/IP Gateway, the Client Logging, and Access Control by selecting the appropriate check boxes.

8. Verify the DNS addressing information for the domain and name server by checking the information that appears against your own notes (where you've recorded this information earlier, prior to installation).

9. Back out by pressing Escape lots of times; then reboot the computer.

Any TCP/IP details not configured when TCP/IP was enabled must be fixed during this installation, or your gateway won't work.

Providing client access to an IPX/IP Gateway

To enable client access to the outside TCP/IP network under control of NDS, follow these steps:

1. Add the NWADMIN snap-ins for the IPX/IP Gateway for your version of the management station client and NetWare.

The steps for adding these snap-ins vary depending on several factors, so check the README files for details.

2. Open the amended NWADMIN program as supervisor or equivalent.

3. Highlight the users, groups, or containers to modify and press Enter.

4. Click the IPX/IP Gateway Service Restrictions button and set the access level that you prefer. This can range from completely free and unfettered access to the Internet at large, to imposing a set of filters that limits access only to "legitimate" sources of business information.

5. Click OK to save the changes.

Take a good look at all the choices in NWADMIN to control Internet access. You and your management must find a level of access that enables people to do their work while keeping them from frittering away the workday mindlessly surfing. Good luck.

Using IPTUNNEL for IPX encapsulation

One of the earliest Internet connections Novell servers made was to package IPX inside TCP/IP packets to send NetWare traffic across the Internet. The encapsulation of IPX within TCP/IP provided some security against prying, and represented an early implementation of a *VPN* (Virtual Private Network).

To configure your NetWare server to communicate over IPTUNNEL, perform the following steps:

1. Type **LOAD INETCFG** at the server console's colon prompt.

2. Choose Boards from the main menu, highlight the board supporting TCP/IP, and then press Insert.

3. Choose IPTUNNEL from the Available Drivers list that appears.

4. Name the board something unique but descriptive; provide the peer server address (you must obtain this information in advance from your own IP address database, an Internet Service Provider, or another network administrator); give the local server address.

5. Press Escape to save and then choose Bindings from the main menu.

6. Bind IPX to the IPTUNNEL driver.

Choose IPX in the Protocols listing, IPTUNNEL in the drivers listing, and then click the Bind button.

7. Press Escape to save and exit.

8. Reboot the server to load the IPTUNNEL server modules.

This system assumes you're programming another server exactly like this one, except that the local and remote server addresses are different. To communicate over IPTUNNEL, each NetWare server must have a full-time Internet connection ready to go at any time.

Management utilities and users see the remote server, and that server works just like other servers in the NDS tree do. Of course, it's remote and, therefore, slower to reach and respond to user requests, but that's not a serious problem, given that connectivity is usually more important than performance when accessing remote resources.

Installing NetWare/IP

For those with pre-NetWare 5 NetWare, NetWare/IP is the only way to get full TCP/IP support between client and server. If you thought adding the IPX/IP Gateway was a pain, you'll reconsider soon. Novell needed to clean up the client-to-server TCP/IP process, and it did a good job in NetWare 5. If you really want an all-TCP/IP network, you'll save time, money, and aggravation by upgrading to NetWare 5. If you don't upgrade, don't come crying to us about the NetWare/IP hassles.

There are four critical pieces to NetWare/IP support:

+ TCP/IP support at the server

+ Configuration of the special NetWare/IP control files

+ TCP/IP added to the client

+ A link between TCP/IP and IPX-based NetWare networks so everyone on both sides and both protocols can remain part of one network

You should now have added TCP/IP support to the server. See the "Configuring and using TCP/IP" section for more details. Verify that your server is still supporting TCP/IP by using the PING command from another TCP/IP station and making sure your NetWare server responds.

Now you must configure the NetWare server so it will accept NetWare clients over TCP/IP rather than IPX. During NetWare/IP installation, you are given a chance to add TCP/IP support to the server as part of the NetWare/IP installation process. Don't believe that lie. If TCP/IP isn't up and running on your server before you start to install NetWare/IP, you will have no joy and much frustration.

1. Type **LOAD INSTALL** at the server console colon prompt.

2. Choose Products⇨NetWare/IP.

3. Provide the source of the NetWare/IP program files (usually your server CD-ROM drive).

4. Let the files load, and then exit.

Sure, you can configure NetWare/IP the way Novell says in the manual, or rather, you can try to configure it our way. Our way is better, believe me. Next, we configure DNS (Domain Name Service), the Internet method for tracking and finding addresses. DNS resolves symbolic domain names like www.novell.com to numeric IP addresses like 137.65.2.5, and can even perform reverse lookups (to make sure the numeric address corresponds to the symbolic name that a would-be user provides to the DNS).

DNS provides an important service that enables the global reach built into the Internet. For more information, please consult the text of RFCs 1101, 1183, and 1637 (you may read any or all of these online at www.cis.ohio-state.edu/rfc/rfcnnnn.txt by replacing the nnnn in the preceding string with the four-digit RFC number for whichever RFC you wish to read).

When it comes to configuring DNS on NetWare, please follow these steps:

1. Type **LOAD UNICON** at the server console colon prompt.

2. Provide your ADMIN username and password in the Server Login window.

3. In UNICON's main menu, choose Manage Services⇨ Manage Master Database⇨Initialize DNS Master Database.

4. Press Escape until you return to the main UNICON menu.

5. Choose Manage Services⇨NetWare/IP⇨Configure Primary DSS.

6. Provide a name for your Domain Sap Server (DSS) that substitutes for the automatic application support in IPX that's missing from TCP/IP.

Be sure to add nwip. (dot) to the beginning of the name displayed in the NetWare/IP Domain: field, or it won't work.

7. Press Escape until you return to the main UNICON menu.

8. Choose Configure NetWare/IP Server.

9. Provide the name of your NetWare/IP domain (again) and the DSS name (again), and say YES to the Forward IPX Information to DSS? Question at the bottom of the current window.

10. Press Escape until you return to the main UNICON menu.

11. Choose Start/Stop Services⇨Start NetWare/IP.

12. Shout for joy if no error message appears; you're finished at the server.

If error messages do appear, you have no choice but to consult the online documentation for an explanation of the error. In some cases, you may need to start the DSS installation all over again. Be sure to check each and every values along the way and make sure it's correct. Incorrect or invalid values (typos, basically) are the bane of many a DSS configuration!

Configuring the NetWare client software for Client32 stations is much simpler: Redo the installation process, but this time check the TCP/IP box. This makes the NetWare/IP box active, and you must check it. Then reinstall the client, as described in Part III.

Installing the Web Server

NetWare 4.11 shipped with Novell's own (licensed) Web server, and it was a decent Web server. Then Novell started a joint partnership with Netscape, called Novonyx, and that small group ported the Netscape product line to run on NetWare servers. Goodbye, NetWare Web server; hello, Netscape FastTrack Web Server for NetWare.

NetWare 5 is the first standard NetWare product to include the Netscape FastTrack server, but you don't need to stick with the older NetWare Web server if you're still running an earlier version of NetWare. Novell's Web site offers the Netscape/NetWare FastTrack Web server free for downloading. Take this opportunity to turn a NetWare server into a fire-breathing Web server — and for free, too.

Here are your instructions for installing the Netscape FastTrack Web server:

1. On a workstation that's logged in to the server under the name ADMIN or the equivalent, load the CD-ROM that contains the Netscape source files.

2. If you downloaded the files from the Novell Web server, make the directory where those files reside your current directory. (Type **CD** *<directory-name>*, but replace *<directory name>* with the name of the directory where the files reside.)

3. Type **SETUP** from the root of the CD-ROM directory or the hard disk directory that holds the downloaded files.

4. Click the Finish button.

Not too hard, is it? Netscape's FastTrack server is completely integrated with NDS, so you now have complete control of the Web server through NWADMIN without doing another thing.

Using the Web manager

You need a workstation equipped with a Web browser to perform Netscape administration. Because NetWare includes the Netscape Web client software, you should be ready for this.

During installation, you supply a unique port number for your Web server. To perform administration on this Web server, you must type the following line as a *URL* (Uniform Resource Locator) or a Web address:

```
http://servername:portnumber/
```

The server name may be either the name you assign during installation or the IP address of the host NetWare server. The port number must match the number you gave during installation or you end up with the computer equivalent of locking your keys in your car: You're almost there, but you can't get in.

The General Administration buttons across the front of the Web server offer the following choices:

✦ **Admin Preferences:** These control the layout and capabilities of the Administrator display that governs the administrative interface to the Web server.

✦ **Global Settings:** These define the kinds of display and access controls to Web pages, applications, and services that apply to all users of a site.

✦ **Users & Groups:** These permit an Administrator to manage access to specific resources and Web pages on the basis of user accounts and named groups.

✦ **Keys & Certificates:** These provide access to specific public and private keys, for user authentication, and certificates, to present as proof of the validity of site services, addresses, and names.

✦ **Cluster Management:** This provides an interface to manage collections of servers, known as clusters, that aggregate to provide a higher level of data and service access than a single server could provide.

Click the ON or OFF button on the front page of Server Manager to start or stop the Web server.

For detailed help in configuring your new Netscape FastTrack Web Server software, see any of the Netscape Web server documentation that comes with the Web server software itself, the Netscape home Web server, or the Novell Web server.

How to Get Help When You Need It Most

If your network — or the software that runs on your network — breaks, you may sometimes need professional help. Your odds of a successful "technical-support experience" are much more favorable if you know how to communicate with vendors' support organizations and know how to play the game on their terms and win.

This appendix is a quick reference on how to interact effectively with technical-support organizations. It explains how to become an effective communicator with support professionals and tells you how to gather the information you need to answer their questions. Better still, this appendix provides some brief but cogent advice on how to work with technical-support people. It also tries to explain what kind of support you should expect to receive and what to do if the support that you receive fails to satisfy your expectations.

Assembling the Information

Before anyone else can help you with a problem, you must first
figure out enough of what's going on around you to describe your
problems in a meaningful way. In the following sections, you find
out how to correctly document your difficulties and what
maintaining a ready-to-use set of descriptions of what's out there
on your network actually involves.

Know what you're dealing with

As you organize any network or the applications that it delivers,
building a list of the equipment you own is always a good idea.
You can do so by using a variety of software and network-
inventory packages if you want, but plain paper and pencil
usually suffice quite nicely. Documenting a network is a monoto-
nous but demanding task — if the chips are down, you really
have no acceptable substitute for an accurate network and
software inventory. Doing without such an inventory is like trying
to make an insurance claim after a twister carries your trailer off
to Oz — without providing a list of the trailer's contents.

For your inventory, you want to take notes about

+ Each of the adapters on your network

+ Your file servers and their configurations

+ Each desktop machine and the applications that each user
operates

The following list enumerates what kinds of equipment and
software should appear in your inventory:

+ Cable plant (type, length, location, end-labels)

+ Disk storage

+ File server

+ Software running on each workstation

+ Tape-backup unit

+ Workstations

Serving up all the details

For each file server in your organization, you must document its
equipment, software, and characteristics. Take notes on the
following information:

+ How much RAM each machine has installed
+ The number of disk drives and their capacities
+ The network adapters in use
+ The make, model, and configuration data for the disk controller or controllers
+ Which kind of monitor, mouse, and keyboard are attached

Here's the steps you should follow:

1. Record this information for each and every file server under your purview. Fill in the blanks and save this information where you can find it if you need it. Save another copy off-site so that you have a copy even if a twister should hit.

2. Complete the same exercise for each desktop machine on your network. Add the contents of each machine's configuration files. (For DOS, Windows 95, or Windows 98, these files would be AUTOEXEC.BAT and CONFIG.SYS, plus the various Registry files.) For Windows NT, complement your paper documents with an Emergency Repair Disk, a recent Registry backup, and a complete system backup for each NT machine.

3. Document your LAN's software configuration. Obtain listings of each NetWare server's AUTOEXEC.NCF and STARTUP.NCF files and record information about all the following items:

  • Application structure, as the NetWare Application Launcher manages it

  • Directory structure of the file server

  • Drive mappings

  • Network printer information, plus descriptions of other network-accessible devices

  • File and directory attributes and rights for each user and group

  • Groups on the LAN

  • System login script

  • Usernames on the LAN and their network addresses

Whenever you encounter a problem, always write down what happened immediately before that problem manifested itself. Recording any changes that you make to files or hardware is especially important, whether they cause problems or not. (If you don't, your configuration data doesn't remain current very long.) Write down whatever error messages appear to inform you that things aren't going quite right. Write down what you were doing or what the system was doing at the time the problem popped up. If you call a technical-support hot line, the folks who work there almost always ask for this information. If you've got it ready, you save time, look more professional, and get the help you need that much faster.

Beckoning for Help

After you gather the necessary information to document your working environment and the problem you're trying to solve, you can take a deep breath and call for technical support. In the following sections, you find out about the most likely outcomes of your first call on any technical support operation and how to climb the chain of command if you can't get the kind of help you need from the first line of support you encounter in your quest for assistance.

Tech support by the numbers

After you document your systems and networks fully, if something goes wrong, you're totally equipped to take on nearly any vendor's technical support staff. As you make your first call for help, have this information ready. But also prepare yourself for one of the following five things to happen:

✦ You sit on hold for what seems like forever, and after you do get through to the hot line, your only option is to leave voice mail.

✦ You're told that your problem is an operator error. *Operator error* is a general term that tech support professionals use as a euphemism for "user mistake," but the term may also crop up if a tech support person doesn't want to deal with your question or if an answer is not readily apparent.

✦ You're told that no one has ever done anything this stupid before. Stick to your guns: Even if you or your users have boldly erred where no one has erred before, the technical-support person's job is still the same — to help you out of your jam, no matter how boneheaded it may seem (or be).

✦ The person you talk to doesn't know the answer but tells you that "someone else will get back to you to solve your problem."

✦ Some nice individual helps you resolve your problem.

Before you call, gather all your lists of information together. Get close to the machine where the problem resides so that you can lead your tech-support person through the information that the support person needs by quoting whatever error messages appear (if, for example, you're trying to duplicate the problem).

Ascending the chain of command

If you get someone on the phone who doesn't want to help, act as you would whenever you have a problem with your gas or electric bill. Ask to speak to a supervisor — in tech support jargon, this tactic is known as "escalating a call." After all, you paid for the product and perhaps even for a support contract, so you should get results!

The same technique works if technical-support people don't call back within a reasonable amount of time — 24 hours after any call is a reasonable time in which to expect a return call, unless the vendor has already established a clear policy that return calls may sometimes take longer (think "holiday weekend"). Call again and leave a message. Keep records for each technical support call that you make, including the time you first call and how long it takes to get a call-back. Keep good records: Get the person's name and direct line (if you can) and write down as much as you can about what you ask and what kinds of replies you get to your questions. This situation is one in which writers' cramp now may come in handy later on.

Some vendors offer technical support 24 hours a day, 7 days a week. Whenever you buy products, ask about the vendor's technical-support capabilities. Paying extra at the time you buy a product may be worth the cost if you can obtain good support after the sale.

Twenty-four-hour support is vital for network hardware and software. Nobody takes down a network during working hours to insert a new network adapter in a server or to upgrade server software. If you need to work late to accommodate users' needs for prime-time network access, the person on the other end of the line should be available when you need them most.

Where to Find the Answers

Concerning help with NetWare, you may have more sources of help than you expect. In addition to the obvious source of help — Novell itself — third parties can also help with your difficulties. Then, too, NetWare self-help groups and special technical publications also are available if only you know where to look for them. You find out about some of your options in all these areas in the following sections.

800-NETWARE and 900-SUPPORT

We have a thing about "cute" phone numbers, but at least they're easy to remember — they're just hard to dial. These two numbers get you to Novell's customer service department (800-NETWARE, or 800-338-9273) and an independent, for-hire technical-support company (900-SUPPORT, or 900-787-7678). Novell can help with questions about NetWare, but you must be ready with a credit-card number or support-contract information to obtain their services; 900-SUPPORT can handle questions of any kind. Both cost real money, so have a credit card handy if you call.

If this kind of help sounds appealing, remember that you must be older than 21 to use most 900 numbers (just kidding!). More importantly, you should be aware that some companies — perhaps even your own — block access to all 900 numbers in programming their phone systems. Unless you have a cellular phone that enables you to access 900 lines, you'd be crazy to depend on a 900 number to support your network. Because you don't want to figure out this fact only after the network is down, you may even consider checking out alternatives ahead of time.

The Technical Support Alliance

In 1992, Novell organized a vendor group called the *Technical Support Alliance (TSA)* to provide better support for users and to help users avoid what's often called the "finger-pointing problem" in the tech support game. (This problem occurs if a network contains products from Vendor A and Vendor B; if you report a problem for such a network, Vendor A claims it's Vendor B's fault, and Vendor B claims it's Vendor A's fault. This sort of buck-passing can make resolving problems incredibly difficult.)

Today, the TSA is also known as the *TSA Network,* or *TSANet* for short. TSANet is a group of 81 vendors who cross-train each other in the use of their products. If you call a TSANet member about a problem that may involve several vendors' products, you can get an answer from that vendor with a single phone call. You can visit the TSANet Web site at www.tsanet.org/ for the latest information about member companies, services, and capabilities.

AppNotes and other goodies

AppNotes is what people in the know call Novell's monthly publication, officially called *Novell Application Notes. AppNotes* provides in-depth information about a variety of NetWare-related topics. Call 800-NETWARE for more information about these publications. Get your checkbook or credit card out: *AppNotes* costs $150 a year for a subscription, but it's worth the outlay.

For our money, yet another great reason to upgrade to NetWare 5 is the search engine that comes with the online documentation. Keyword searches make finding — and getting right to — topics and information you never dreamed of easy. You can enter the text for a mysterious error message, for example, and, with a little luck, find out exactly what it means.

NetWare Users International

If you're seriously interested in NetWare and related technologies, you may want to join a local NetWare user group in your area. *NetWare Users International (NUI)* is affiliated with Novell. You can find out whether a chapter's in your area by calling the universal NetWare number: 800-NETWARE. On the Web, NUI appears as an entry in the site map at www.novell.com; as of this writing, the NUI home page is at webapps.novell.com/nui/.

Online is where the action is

Lots of places online can provide help if things on your network get really weird. For NetWare, among the best of these places is the Novell Web site, which is Novell's online information service. (See Appendix B for the details.) Aside from online information services such as AOL, CompuServe, and so forth, many companies operate their own bulletin boards, where you can leave questions or get copies of new drivers, bug fixes, and other things. If you have an Internet connection and enough time, you can find out about almost anything network-related.

Books and courses for everyone

Books that explain NetWare's inner workings and its wiles and ways are also readily available, as well as classes where you can find out more about NetWare than you imagined possible. At a bare minimum, we recommend checking out our companion book — namely, *Networking With NetWare For Dummies*, 4th Edition (IDG Books Worldwide, Inc.). Novell also sanctions publications from Novell Press that offer lots of useful NetWare-related information.

Look in networking magazines for NetWare training and education centers in your city. Check out computer and networking magazines, too, and look in your local bookstore: More information about networking and NetWare is available at reasonable prices than you may ever guess.

If you take any NetWare-related training classes, you may decide that you also want to take the certification route. Novell defines several certified NetWare Professional programs, wherein, by following certain curricula, you can become a certified NetWare administrator (CNA), a certified NetWare engineer (CNE), or perhaps even a Master CNE (MCNE).

If you're a casual user on a network, these credentials really aren't right for your needs and probably represent more time, effort, and expense than you're inclined to lay out. But if you manage a network in the workplace, you may consider tackling one or more of these certifications. The CNA covers network administration and involves taking at least three courses and passing an equal number of tests. The CNE is for people who not only must cope with NetWare (creating users, for example), but who must also work with network hardware. The Master CNE program offers specializations in network management, infrastructure and advanced access, intranet technologies, or groupware integration. The CNE and MCNE are for individuals who consider NetWare system management their career focus.

If you're interested in finding out more about Novell's certification and training offerings, make sure you visit the Training & Services area at www.novell.com (or just jump straight to www.novell.com/programs/). Also, while you're shopping around for NetWare training, be aware that Novell licenses its own training materials to qualified training operations, known as Novell Authorized Education Centers (NAECs). If you're looking for the best, most up-to-date information (but not necessarily the cheapest offerings), NAECs are an excellent source for NetWare-related classroom training. Although many training companies offer such training, only NAECs can claim to operate with a Novell seal of approval (which can make a profound difference in the quality of training you receive).

NetWare Information Online

This appendix takes aim at the copious volumes of
NetWare information and support available on the
Internet. We show you how to find the information
and support you need to make a NetWare network
hum (or least, to help restore it to its former condition,
whatever that may have been). We also describe the
limits to what you should expect to find online and
when you may be better served by direct phone
support for NetWare problems. The explosive growth
of the Internet and World Wide Web sites means that
Novell (and nearly every other major computer vendor)
concentrates its support efforts on the Internet rather
than on proprietary online systems such as America
Online (AOL) and CompuServe.

The Best Sources for NetWare Information

The primo place for NetWare information these days (and where to contact Novell's online support) is the Novell Web site, at `www.novell.com`. Lots of Internet Web sites besides `www.novell.com`, however, also contain NetWare information and support data, files, and self-help materials. Numerous Usenet newsgroups, the Internet equivalent of the old CompuServe NetWire forums, are also available. Through such newsgroups, you can ask NetWare-related questions and get answers not only from real NetWare support professionals, but also from other users who've picked up NetWare's secrets in the school of hard knocks.

For the sake of this discussion, we assume that you already know the basics of Internet navigation and how to configure a news reader for Usenet newsgroups. If our assumption is wrong, check out *The Internet For Dummies,* 4th Edition, by John Levine (IDG Books Worldwide, Inc.); it has the space to cover the necessary details that we can't give you in this paltry appendix!

www.novell.com: Novell's Web at your service

World Wide Web sites are dynamic by their nature. That's why we can't guarantee that the Novell Web page that appears as we write this appendix is the same one you see when you visit their site for yourself. Rest assured that, although the details always change over time, you can get product information, search the site's numerous Web pages, and search the Novell KnowledgeBase for technical information. The current choices available to you after you arrive at `www.novell.com` are:

✦ **Products:** The current crop of Novell product offerings.

✦ **Technical Support:** This section enables you to search for files, updates, and technical support documents; explore job opportunities in Novell Technical Support; and explore the different support options offered by Novell.

✦ **Partners:** Information about Novell's partnering programs; aimed primarily at vendors who offer complementary or NetWare-enabled products — but informative for users and NetWare administrators alike.

✦ **Developers:** Everything you ever wanted to know about developing NetWare applications, plus access to information, tools, downloads, and other cool stuff.

✦ **Company Information:** The hub of the universe for all things Novell related, from quarterly reports to press releases, news clippings, and more.

✦ **Training & Services**: Find out how to become a certified NetWare engineer or instructor; locate the Novell authorized education center nearest you.

✦ **Promotions & Events:** Information about Novell's developer conference, BrainShare, trade shows that the company attends, and road shows and other seminars coming to a hotel in a town near you!

✦ **Year 2000:** Novell's information about Y2K issues, capabilities, and potential problems that users of older NetWare versions may face. A must-visit site for organizations concerned about Y2K compliance and potential problems.

✦ **International Sites:** An online index to international sources of NetWare information around the world, aimed primarily at non-English-speaking audiences.

The KnowledgeBase search

To our way of thinking, the KnowledgeBase search is one of the most useful — and most-used — areas of the Novell Web site. Visit the Novell KnowledgeBase to glom onto every technical detail relating to NetWare support. If you, or anyone else, ever calls NetWare's telephone support staff about some pesky problem with a NetWare network, one result of that call, assuming that it concerns a new or heretofore unreported problem, is the production of a corresponding document in the KnowledgeBase.

The production of such documents explains why the Novell KnowledgeBase is a treasure trove of information about known bugs, previously reported problems, and unique problems (and solutions) that people have reported already to Novell's technical support operation. This setup also means that you can benefit from the experience of hundreds of thousands of other NetWare users without needing to talk to each one personally. So, the KnowledgeBase is the first place you should look for help on just about any topic, because the odds are extremely good — unless you're dealing with beta software — that somebody else found and solved the problem before you encountered it.

Novell also places a document in the KnowledgeBase every time it releases a new bug fix, file update, or new release to the public. That's why KnowledgeBase searches can return technical advice and specific filenames that may help rectify whatever problems you may be trying to solve. We always start with a KnowledgeBase search as our first step toward resolving unusual problems that don't appear in other NetWare documentation. We suggest that you put a KnowledgeBase search high on your priority list for resolving problems, too.

Miles and Miles of Files and Smiles

Many of the documents in the KnowledgeBase specify that you should download an updated file or patch to resolve common NetWare problems. If you do come across such a recommendation, you can click the name of the file directly on the KnowledgeBase document page, and get instructions on how to download the file on the spot.

But, say that your Uncle Vern was telling you about a new update for the NetWare CLIB NLMs, and you reckon that you simply *must* have it on your own server. The quickest way to find that new CLIB update is to go to the Novell Web page at www.novell.com, click the Search icon at the top of the page, enter the keyword **CLIB** in the Search for Software Updates, Patches, and Drivers in Novell's File Finder field. You go directly to the file. Single-click the filename, and it downloads in a matter of minutes. Uncle Vern would be *so* proud that a smile would certainly cross his old and wrinkly face.

If you happen to be a Unix guru, you may be more at home in the clutches of the Novell FTP server than in those of the slick Novell Web pages. You're in luck! You can download bug fixes, updates, and new file releases through ftp.novell.com. Bring on the command line!

Other Web Resources for NetWare Information

Besides Novell's own Web-based resources, lots of other places are available for seeking out NetWare-related information online. In the following sections, you get a quick briefing on Usenet and some tasty mailing lists, plus pointers to vendor Web sites that can prove real treasure troves of NetWare information.

Usenet and mailing lists

As you discover through a quick visit to www.novell.com, a plethora of information on NetWare is available from the Novell Web site. But wait — there's more! First off, the Web site offers a discussion about Usenet, called comp.os.netware, where you can ask direct questions of the teeming masses of NetWare nerds around the world. Under this part of the newsgroup hierarchy, you also find the following newsgroups:

✦ comp.os.netware.announce: Check here for NetWare-related news, events, and product announcements.

✦ comp.os.netware.connectivity: Check here for net-working and other connectivity information specifically related to NetWare.

- ✦ `comp.os.netware.misc`: Check here for topics that the other members of the comp.os.netware newsgroups don't cover.

- ✦ `comp.os.netware.security`: Check here for information about NetWare and security matters.

Usenet is always our second line of defense if we have a really unusual situation that none of the Novell KnowledgeBase documents cover. Usenet newsgroups have more NetWare experts than you can shake a stick at. One of them can offer the solution to your problem, point you in the right direction, or at least commiserate with you in your network doldrums. Don't be afraid to dive into the discussion. The only dumb questions are the ones that you don't ask!

On the other hand, lots of specialized mailing lists, some of which are devoted to NetWare, are also on the Internet. You can find NetWare lists with special concerns, such as the NetWare Hack Mailing List at the following URL:

`www.fastlane.net/~thegnome/compute/nwhack1/`

Then, too, lots of user groups have their own mailing lists. One good example is the Kansas Valley NetWare Users Group, KawNUG, at the following address:

`kawnug.oznet.ksu.edu/about/about.htm`

In general, you can find lots of NetWare-related mailing lists, with the right kinds of topical (and perhaps even regional) focus by visiting a search engine (such as `www.yahoo.com`, `www.excite.com`, `www.altavista.digital.com`, and so forth). We found the following search string to be particularly helpful in locating useful pointers to mailing lists:

`"NetWare" AND "mailing list"`

Manufacturers' Web pages

Another excellent route to NetWare technical support is through other manufacturers' Web sites. Nearly every major network adapter manufacturer, SCSI adapter manufacturer, hard-drive manufacturer, NetWare software developer, and server manufacturer has a Web page that contains technical information and the latest drivers for that company's particular NetWare-related products. These manufacturers' sites can be an excellent source of hardware and software specific information. You can use an Internet search engine such as Yahoo! at `www.yahoo.com` or AltaVista at `www.altavista.digital.com` to locate home pages for major hardware and software manufacturers. Simply use the manufacturer's name in the search engine or, if you're feeling adventurous, try typing **www.*manufacturer*.com** (where *manufacturer* is the company's name) in your Web browser's URL window. (For many companies, this type of address is all you need to get to their Web sites.)

Techie Talk

Access Control: The list of restrictions that defines your permissions to resources on the network.

account: Have you ever opened a checking account at a bank? Certain restrictions exist and a variety of plans are available, all aimed at making you "accountable." The account each user has on the LAN works the same way.

adapter: Similar in function to the ignition switch on a car, the adapter gets workstations talking on the LAN. Placed in a workstation's bus, the adapter communicates requests between the workstation and the physical media (such as twisted-pair cabling) that connects the LAN.

ADMIN: ADMIN is one of the top positions on the directory tree. It has access to the root of the directory tree. ADMIN can, therefore, create the network's initial directory structure and create administrators to manage segments, or partitions, of the directory tree. Or ADMIN can create a portion of the initial structure and have partition managers create the rest.

administrator rights: Those rights that let you do everything on the network. They're called administrator rights because they give you the same access as the ADMIN user.

administrator equivalent: Has the same rights as the ADMIN user.

aliases: Not everyone has an alias. If you've ever been on the other side of the law, however, you probably know someone who does. In NetWare 4.*x* and higher, objects can have alternative names, or aliases, that help to identify them.

AppleTalk: The name of the set of protocols that the folks at Apple Computer developed. Apple's Macintosh was one of the first mass-market computers to offer built-in networking capabilities. In most cases, where you find a Mac, you also find AppleTalk.

applications: A software program used by the available network resources. A network without applications is similar to having a car and nowhere to go. Word-processing programs, spreadsheets, and e-mail are examples of applications.

archive: The process of removing old files from the server so you have room for vibrant and fresh new files. If you ever want any of the old dogs back, you can unarchive them. Archive media can be CD-ROM, WORM, RAID, or simply tape.

ATM (Asynchronous Transfer Mode): A high-speed transmission method that uses a fixed-size packet.

attach: What you do to connect to a server other than the one into which you're currently logged. In NetWare 4.*x* and higher, you use LOGIN /NS.

attributes: The characteristics that define what users can do to the files and directories that NetWare manages. Attributes vary by user or group and affect whether you can copy, delete, execute, or modify a file (and so on).

AUTOEXEC.BAT: The file containing the commands that enable you to start your computer in the manner you want. You load the NIC driver in this file, and you can put the LOGIN command in it.

AUTOEXEC.NCF: You can use this file to boot the server, just as you can the AUTOEXEC.BAT file. AUTOEXEC.NCF enables you to load the server drivers and any NLMs the network operating system uses.

backbone: A network backbone connects file servers in a single, unified "internetwork." If your network gets a slipped disk, it's just as incapacitating as the real thing if it happens to your back.

backup: This term has nothing to do with raising your hackles, but you may actually do so if you don't perform one of these. This term refers to the files created when you back up your LAN every night: saving the files on the network to some form of offline storage.

baseline: Gives you a snapshot of the network to establish how normal activity patterns look. Setting a baseline involves capturing statistics that describe how people use the network throughout the course of a normal working day.

Bindery: A database used by NetWare 3.*x* that contains information about the users, groups, and devices on the LAN, such as printers.

boot: What you do to your workstation as you turn it on or to the server as you load SERVER.EXE.

BorderManager: Novell's Internet security server, or proxy server. You use to make sure that, if you connect your company to the Internet, local users can get out, but remote users can't get in.

cache: Squirrels cache nuts so they can eat them in the winter. Like squirrels, NetWare stores data in caches so the program can get to that data quickly later.

CAPTURE: A NetWare print utility that redirects local printer ports to network printers.

CD-ROM: A storage device similar to the CD you may have at home that plays Alanis Morissette (but is less inflammatory). A CD-ROM stores only the data you think is important enough to save.

client: A desktop machine is a client on the network, or simply a client. Calling the machine a desktop focuses on its role in supporting an individual, who typically is working at a desk; calling it a client focuses on its network connection. Whatever you call your computer, it's still the same thing — the machine you sit in front of while you work.

communications: Communications protocols establish the rules for how computers talk to each other or what things mean.

compression: A mathematical technique for analyzing computer files to squeeze them down to a smaller size. A feature of most backup systems, compression is available in NetWare 4.*x* and higher. These versions can compress files that you store on the file server. According to Novell, this kind of file compression can result in an increase in storage capacity that's better than two to one.

CONFIG.SYS: See your DOS manual for an explanation. (This is a NetWare book.)

connection number: After a device logs in to the file server, it receives a connection number, which the network then uses to identify that device's ongoing network session. The connection number thus serves as a way of directing replies back to the device to satisfy that device's requests for network services.

connections: The connections include the physical pieces of gear you need to hook up a computer to the network, plus the wires or other materials — known as the networking medium — that the network uses to carry messages from one computer to another or among multiple computers.

console operator: This person has the authority to use the file-server console.

console: The monitor attached to the file server. You can access the console remotely using the RCONSOLE command or across a modem line using the ACONSOLE command. You run special NetWare commands, known as console commands, from the server keyboard.

ConsoleOne: NetWare 5's new Java-based GUI administration tool for the server.

containers and container objects: Just as you use that storage area behind the stairs (the container) to store things (container objects), you organize objects into containers in NetWare 4.x and higher Directory Services.

context: In NetWare 4.x and higher, each object has a context that identifies its location in the directory tree. An object's context is important; taken out of context, it has no meaning.

default server: If the default drive is the one you log in to, what do you think the default server is? That's right — it's the server you log in to. If your file server is the only file server on the LAN, it's also the default server.

Directory Service Manager for NetWare: An application available from Microsoft that lets a Windows NT Server control an NDS database.

Directory tree: Another name for the structure of the NDS database (because it looks like a tree).

directory: Similar to the Yellow Pages. Although directories aren't alphabetical, they organize the files on a file-server volume. Not to be confused with the NetWare Directory that NetWare Directory Services maintains on 4.x and higher-numbered versions of NetWare.

distributed: In more than one place, like the NDS keeps pieces of the security database all over the network.

drive mapping: When you map a drive, you give the system instructions so you can find that drive again quickly. Most users have maps to their default directories, to their MAIL directories, and to the PUBLIC directory.

driver: The guy behind the wheel of a LAN adapter.

EGP Filters: A set of filters defined through FILTCFG that control how the Exterior Gateway Protocol operates.

encryption: Shhh! Like a secret code, encryption is a way of making sure that no one is able to read the information you're sending across the network except the person for whom it's destined.

Ethernet: Everyone's all-time favorite network-access method.

EVERYONE: A group created automatically when you install NetWare. EVERYONE is a good catch-all group into which you can put everyone who should have the same access to all the same applications.

File and Print Services for NetWare: See *FPNW.*

file caching: See *cache.*

file server: The device on a network that services requests from the workstations.

file system: The way in which the network operating system handles and stores files.

File Transfer Protocol: See *FTP.*

FILER: NetWare's built-in file- and directory-management tool, available to both end users and administrators. You can use it to move, delete, or rename files and directories; to review attributes and rights; and to navigate around the file structures on NetWare servers.

firewall: A hardware or software device used to protect a local network from intruders (like those wild boys on the Internet).

FPNW (File and Print Services for NetWare): Allows NetWare clients to access resources on a Windows NT Server without installing additional software on the client.

FTP (File Transfer Protocol): The TCP/IP protocol suite includes a file-transfer program named FTP, which can copy files between any two TCP/IP-equipped computers.

gateway: An electronic or software device that connects two or more dissimilar computer systems. A NetWare-to-IBM-mainframe gateway, for example, takes the IPX from one side of the gateway and translates it to the SNA protocol that some IBM mainframe communications require. Gateways are becoming more and more common as vendors figure out how to make this computer talk to that computer.

Graphical User Interface: See *GUI.*

GSNW (Gateway Services for NetWare): Allows Windows clients to access NetWare resources through a Windows NT Server without loading additional software on the client.

GUEST: An account assigned to someone visiting your network. You know what this term means — that you must be polite and follow the rules, because your visit to the network is only temporary.

GUI (Graphical User Interface): The type of interface with pretty pictures and icons and many, many colors.

HCSS (High-Capacity Storage System): Part of NetWare 4.*x* and higher, HCSS enables NetWare administrators to migrate less frequently accessed data from a server's hard drive to some kind of alternative storage medium, typically a rewritable magneto-optical drive. Because these systems are removable and have large capacities but can retrieve data nearly as fast as conventional disk drives, this type of storage is often called near-line. In contrast, the server's hard drives contain online files that are available almost instantly. After a user requests a file on the near-line system, the file must be copied back from that system to the server's hard drive before it can be accessed (a reverse-migration process). As with file compression, you can have the least-active server files automatically migrate to optical disk according to a selectable age threshold, based on the date of most recent access.

HELP: The program you call if you can't find the explanation in this book.

High-Capacity Storage System: See *HCSS.*

hot swappable: Equipment (almost always hard drives right now) that can be pulled from its server while the server is up and running.

HTTP (HyperText Transfer Protocol): The Internet TCP/IP protocol used to manage communication between Web clients and servers.

Internet Protocol: See *IP.*

intruder detection: The series of measures you can put in place by way of SYSCON that enable you to find and identify the people who are trying to break into the LANs or put their paws on information to which they don't have access.

intruder: Anyone trying to break into the LAN, no matter what her intentions. An intruder may be your boss, who's trying to break into your directories to read your latest invective against him, or someone from outside who's trying to steal company secrets. Most of the time, these people are just plain stupid — in NetWare, you usually have a way to catch them.

IP: The Internet Protocol in the TCP/IP protocol suite, IP does what IPX does in NetWare — it sets up the mechanism for transferring data across the network.

IPX/IP Gateway: A piece of software that runs on a NetWare server that converts information from IPX to IP for transmission over the Internet.

IPX (Internetwork Packet Exchange): NetWare's transport protocol.

Java: Coffee! Also a robust, object-oriented programming language which can run on almost any computer.

Java Virtual Machine: See *JVM.*

Jukebox: "1, 2, 3 o'clock, 4 o'clock rock . . . ." Actually, in computer terminology, it's a piece of hardware that can handle many CD-ROMs and may even change them automatically.

JVM (Java Virtual Machine): A software specification, written in C, that interprets Java programs compiled into byte-codes.

LAN driver: The LAN driver supplies the get-up-and-go and the brains for the NIC.

LAN: A local area network. See also *network.*

leaf object: The directory in NetWare 4.*x* and higher assumes the form of a tree. It has roots, branches, and leaf objects. Leaf objects are the end points of the tree — they can't contain any other objects, and they represent only themselves. Users, volumes, servers, and printers are all leaf objects.

local area network: See *LAN.*

log out: What you do whenever you check out from the LAN.

login script: A file that can either exist individually for each user or serve all users. It contains commands that control the way a user views her desktop. Users can create and edit their own login scripts. Only the supervisor can create and edit the System Login script.

LOGIN: The LOGIN command, well, logs you in to the system.

NAL (NetWare Application Launcher): A small program that runs on Windows systems which enables administrators to control the programs to which users have access.

name space: Each time you want to add a different type of machine, such as a Macintosh, an OS/2-based machine, or a UNIX-based machine, you must provide for file compatibility with NetWare. You do so through the name spaces you load on the file server as NLMs to regulate the cross-network conversion that must take place.

NCP (NetWare Core Protocol): An NCP is the service protocol for NetWare. Virtually every service NetWare can provide has an NCP it uses to enable users to send requests for, and receive delivery of, services. The services that the NetWare NCPs provide range from file transfer to directory services lookups.

NDS (NetWare Directory Services): NDS is NetWare's approach to joining lots of LANs together without users getting lost. It consists of a database containing all the users, equipment, storage, and other entities on the network. In NDS, users can locate network resources without knowing where these resources are physically located.

NetBEUI: Stands for NetBIOS Extended User Interface; it was designed as a second-generation protocol especially to support NetBIOS-based communications. You can call NetBIOS and NetBEUI a matched set — they are what Microsoft and IBM use for their networking products.

NetBIOS: Stands for Networked Basic Input-Output System, and was designed by IBM as a networked extension to PC BIOS. NetBIOS is a higher-level protocol that runs on top of lots of lower-level protocols, including IPX and TCP/IP. Although NetBIOS is pretty old, it's very easy to program with, and consequently, lots of different networked applications on a broad range of computers and operating systems use it.

NetWare Application Launcher: See *NAL*.

NetWare Core Protocol: See *NCP*.

NetWare Directory Services: See *NDS*.

NetWare Loadable Module: See *NLM*.

network interface card: See *NIC*.

Network Neighborhood: The application in Windows 95, 98, and NT 4.0 that lets you view the available network resources.

network operating system: See *NOS*.

network: A collection of at least two computers linked together so they can communicate with each other.

NFS (Network File System): NFS is the Unix default file sharing network, but with Unix, every system is both a server of its own file system and a client of other file systems.

NIC (Network Interface Card): The gear that hooks up a computer to a network and acts as an intermediary between the computer and the network is called the network interface. (For PCs, it typically comes in the form of an add-in board that everyone calls a network interface card, or NIC.)

NLM (NetWare Loadable Module): A NetWare program that provides low-level operating system access for programs designed to run directly on a server.

node: Any device on the network. A node can be a workstation, a printer, or the file server.

NOS (Network Operating System): The network's main control program is its operating system, because that's the program that enables the network to operate.

object: A directory map object enables the network administrator to define map commands that point to an object rather than to a specific directory on the server. If the path to that object ever changes, you need to update only the object definition, not all your user's MAP commands.

object-oriented: A method that analyzes complex systems (like programs) and focuses on defining data objects and the methods applied to them.

password: The LAN's equivalent to "Open sesame." NetWare enables users to have passwords ranging in length from 1 to 127 alphanumeric characters. Passwords aren't mandatory, but you use them to log on to most networks. We don't recommend the use of overly long passwords. (More than 12 to 15 characters is too difficult to remember.)

pinging: The process of verifying the connectivity between two computers on a network.

PPP (Point to Point Protocol): A modern, low-overhead serial communications protocol, typically used to interconnect two computers via modem.

print queue: NetWare uses print queues to store pending print jobs in the form of print-image files while they wait their turn to print. The queue is the mechanism that handles requests for printing from users and supplies the print-image files to the printer in the correct order. See also *queue.*

print server: The device or software that controls network printing and services printing requests.

properties: John has blue eyes. John works in sales. John is the sales manager. These characteristics of the object "John" are called properties in NetWare 4.*x* and higher.

protocol: In diplomacy, this term refers to the rules for behavior that enable representatives from sovereign governments to communicate with each other in a way calculated to keep things peaceful — or at least under control. The word *protocol* captures the flavor of what these sets of rules do for networks. Most networking protocols consist of a named collection of specific message formats and rules for interaction, rather than a single set of formats and rules. For this reason, protocols are also known as protocol suites, not because they like to lounge around on matched collections of furniture, but because they travel in packs.

queue: See *printer queue.*

RAID (Redundant Array of Inexpensive, or Independent, Disks): It's a hardware or software configuration that ensures data integrity by distributing files over multiple disks.

redirector: A piece of software that looks at each request for service from a user. If the software can satisfy the request locally, it passes that request on to the local PC's operating system to handle. If it can't handle the request locally, it assumes that the request needs to go to the network, and the redirector then passes the request on to a service provider (also known as a server) on the network. Using a redirector is a pretty common way to handle network access from a desktop.

Redundant Array of Inexpensive (or Independent) Disks: See *RAID.*

replication: In NetWare 4.*x* and higher, replication refers to portions of the server or partitions that you copy to other servers.

RIP (Routing Information Protocol): A broadcast protocol (addressed to everyone on a network who's listening) that every IPX router on a network uses one time per minute to declare what it knows about how to get around on the network. (For NetWare v3.11 or higher, any server can be a router.)

router: Routers exchange RIP packets to keep the common knowledge of how a collection of individual networks — known as an internetwork — is laid out. They use this information to move packets around, which is why these servers are known as routers.

Routing Information Protocol: See *RIP.*

SAP (Service Advertising Protocol): Advertises the services available on the network. SAP is a broadcast protocol, and each server sends out its collection of SAPs one time per minute in versions of NetWare earlier than 4.*x*. In NetWare 4.*x* and higher, you can adjust the number of SAPs.

SBACKUP: A backup utility that works with NetWare 5, 4.*x,* and v3.11. As a server-based backup system, it handles DOS, Macintosh, OS/2, and NFS files on workstations or on the server's hard disk. SBACKUP works with a NetWare Loadable Module (NLM), known as the TSA.NLM, to see that data on a target is backed up. The target can be another file server or workstation on the LAN. In case you haven't guessed already, SBACKUP beats the pants off NBACKUP. To run the program, the SUPERVISOR starts SBACKUP from the file-server console.

schema: The master set of rules governing the types of objects in the NetWare 4.*x* and higher directories.

SCSI: SCSI, pronounced "scuzzy," isn't an alternative form of grunge. It's an interface in the computer to which you can attach almost anything, but you mostly attach disk drives.

search drive: Not a charity drive for misplaced things, but rather a drive map you set so you can find files from any drive you're in. Typically, you map search drives to the PUBLIC directory and to any other directories in which you store applications. That way, you can always run your applications and the NetWare commands and utilities, no matter what the current default drive.

Secure Sockets Layer: See *SSL.*

SEND: This command sends the included text to a user or to everyone on your network. Use the ALL option with discretion, however, because that command does what it says — sends the text to everyone on the network.

SERVER.EXE: Everything must start somewhere. The SERVER.EXE file loads the network operating system software onto the file server, naturally.

server: You don't leave tips for servers. They serve low-fat, no-calorie requests to clients, and the only weight they cause you to gain is the amount of information you save in your user directory. The server also stores programs and files for all the workstations in its network. Sometimes, if the amount of data on it becomes too much, you must purge the information from the server.

Service Advertising Protocol: See *SAP.*

servlet: Servlets are to servers as applets are to Java clients. They are part of a network service, usually an HTTP server, that responds to requests from clients.

SETPASS: This command enables you to set a new password for yourself but for no one else.

SFT III: This product is Novell's latest development in server redundancy. (Novell calls it fault tolerance.) It protects information on the server by furnishing multiple storage devices. One method is server mirroring. Server mirroring gives you the ultimate backup plan — if any hardware component in the active server fails, the other machine automatically takes over without any interruption of service. A dedicated network connects the two servers, usually over fiber optic cables, and keeps both servers in synch. Granted, this solution can be expensive, but it's well worth the cost for truly mission-critical environments.

SMP modules: NLMs that support Symmetric MultiProcessing in NetWare 5 servers.

SNA (Systems Network Architecture): IBM's basic protocol suite. Where you find a mainframe or an AS/400, you also typically find SNA. Because SNA was one of the pioneering protocols, companies that invested heavily in mainframe technology in the 1960s and 1970s also invested in building large-scale SNA networks.

SPX: A guaranteed-delivery protocol that NetWare occasionally uses.

SSL (Secure Sockets Layer): A protocol designed by Netscape that provides encrypted communications on the Internet.

STARTUP.NCF: This file resides on the file server and is integral to bringing up the file server.

subnet: A division of an internetwork that limits traffic on the network by dividing it into segments.

SUPERVISOR: The big kahuna of accounts. This is the person in charge.

synchronization: Each server or partition contains a replica of the directory. If something on the network changes, these replicas must get into synch. This process is known as replica synchronization.

SYS:MAIL: You store your mail here after it's sent. Although most of the stuff in this directory is ancient history, don't delete it — it's where your login script is kept.

SYS:PUBLIC: The directory on the default volume (SYS) that contains all the programs that are public (that is, any user can get his hands on them).

SYS:SYSTEM: The directory in which the server stores files necessary for server upkeep and administration, as well as some utilities that are for use by the network supervisor and supervisor equivalents only.

SYSCON: The NetWare 2.*x* and 3.*x* utility that is used to manage users and groups on a server.

system administrator: This person wins and controls all the marbles. This person is also responsible for keeping the servers and the network up and running.

Systems Network Architecture: See *SNA.*

TCP/IP: The real name of this protocol suite is the Transmission Control Protocol and the Internet Protocol. Because the Internet consists of more than 9 million sites worldwide and TCP/IP claims more than 25 million users, it's another major player in the protocol world. TCP/IP has deep roots in the UNIX community and it is also widely used to link computers of different kinds.

time synchronization: Because NDS is time sensitive, time synchronization is used to ensure that all servers in a Directory tree agree on the time.

Transmission Control Protocol/Internet Protocol: See *TCP/IP.*

tree: The NetWare Directory Services hierarchy is called a tree. Directory branches come off the root; leaf objects adorn the end of branches.

trustee rights: Rights of an object to control another object.

Unicode: A 16-bit character standard for uniform character encoding that covers both written characters and text. The Unicode standard is identical to the ISO/IEC 10646-1:1993 ISO standard.

UPS (uninterruptable power supply): A UPS contains a recharge-able battery that provides your server with a backup power source in case its A/C power fails. The UPS senses that A/C power is gone, and it kicks in automatically to supply power to your server on a few milliseconds' notice.

user account: Keeps you in control or enables you to get in trouble on your LAN, depending on whether the supervisor has it in for you.

user: You guessed it — this one is you. It could be someone else, too, but you get the idea.

username: This term refers to you . . . or you . . . or even you. It's your name on the system. Ours are JGASKIN, DJOHNSON, and ETITTEL. See also *user.*

Virtual memory: Space reserved on a computer's hard disk for storing portions of memory.

VLM client software: Software used on DOS clients to connect to NetWare servers.

volume: NetWare divides the file server disks into areas called volumes, which are logical, or nonphysical, divisions of hard disk space.

VREPAIR: Short for Volume Repair, the utility used to fix NetWare volumes.

WAN (wide area network): A network that spans over long distances across nonphysical media, such as satellites, phone lines, and so on.

Web server: A program based on HTTP communications that sends HTML-enabled documents to Web client systems.

workstation: Where you sit, whether you're just a lowly user or the big cheese.

Z.E.N.works: Short for Zero Effort Networks, this is NetWare 5's client management system, which allows you to configure the applications a client sees, change its desktop configuration, and even remotely control a PC.

Index

(continued)

Networking With Netware For Dummies Quick Ref

555555

NDS *(continued)*
Organizational Unit containers, 27
preparing for, 27–28
prerequistes for installing, 40
removing, 143–144
RexxWare Migration Toolkit, 50
root objects, 38
timestamps, 40
Visio's Solution Pack for NDS, 50–51
NETADMIN, 48–49
NETBASIC directory, 23
NET.CFG files, 75
NETINFO.CFG file, 160
Netscape FastTrack Web server, 167
Netscape Navigator, 15
NETUSER utility, 94, 134–135
NetWare
adding TCP/IP protocol, 158–159
built-in routing, 14
client service, 7
configuring DNS (Domain Name Service), 166–167
default directories, 23
defining, 6
file service, 7
history, 6–7
installing, 18–22
Internet Explorer, 15
LANs (Local Area Networks) benefits, 13–14
license utility, 14
loading software modules, 22
migration options from Windows NT, 121–123
Netscape Navigator and, 15
network card support, 8
networks and Internet, 14–15
not built on operating system, 7
operating systems and, 8
print utilities, 51–56
providing services to clients, 6
running applications at server, 6
shutting down, 66–67
version information for components, 76
versions, 9–12
WANs (Wide Area Networks) benefits, 14
NetWare 3.x
32-bit processor, 9
changing menu colors, 102
increased control flexibility, 9
increased server management, 9
installing, 21
MONITOR utility, 132
moving between directories, 102
NLMs (NetWare Loadable Modules), 9
protocol support, 9
recovering deleted files, 102
SETUP command, 21
system login script, 131

tying login scripts to user, 131
user information, 102
NetWare 3.x servers, 120–121
NetWare 4.x, 9–10
additive user licenses, 10
assigning login scripts to container, 131
built-in disk compression, 10
CD-ROM-based installation, 10
graphical utilities, 10
managing network as one entity, 10
MONITOR utility, 132
NDS (NetWare Directory Services), 10
SERVMAN utility, 132
supporting long filenames, 10
TCP/IP support, 10
NetWare 5, 11–12
assigning login scripts to container, 131
installing, 21
migrating Bindery-based networks to, 50
NetWare Administrator, 37, 113, 126–128
See also NWADMIN
NetWare Application Launcher, 11
NetWare Client, 32, 58
NetWare clients, 56–57
connecting to Windows NT Server, 118–120
NetWare Connect, 12
NetWare console, 22
NetWare files, 77
NetWare Hack Mailing List, 181
NetWare High Capacity Storage System, 68–69
NetWare information online, 179–182
NetWare License Diskette, 21
NetWare print services, 51
NetWare servers
activating TCP/IP, 162
adding name-space support to volume, 62–63
adding users and groups, 25–27
booting DOS without memory managers, 22
configuring to accept TCP/IP clients, 165–166
connecting Windows NT Workstation computers to, 115–116
directories, 23, 56
hard drives as local hard drives, 22–23
installation, 141–144
multiple volumes, 23
naming, 21, 53
NDS connectivity, 115
storing data on, 24–25
username, 116
users feeling ownership on, 24–25
viewing all servers in network, 22
NetWare User Tools, 134–135
NetWare v4.11 for Small Business, 13
NetWare/IP, 165–167

(continued)

YOUR ONLINE RESOURCE

WWW.DUMMIES.COM

Discover Dummies Online!

The Dummies Web Site is your fun and friendly online resource for the latest information about ...For Dummies® books and your favorite topics. The Web site is the place to communicate with us, exchange ideas with other ...For Dummies readers, chat with authors, and have fun!

Ten Fun and Useful Things You Can Do at www.dummies.com

1. Win free ...For Dummies books and more!
2. Register your book and be entered in a prize drawing.
3. Meet your favorite authors through the IDG Books Author Chat Series.
4. Exchange helpful information with other ...For Dummies readers.
5. Discover other great ...For Dummies books you must have!
6. Purchase Dummieswear™ exclusively from our Web site.
7. Buy ...For Dummies books online.
8. Talk to us. Make comments, ask questions, get answers!
9. Download free software.
10. Find additional useful resources from authors.

Link directly to these ten
fun and useful things at
http://www.dummies.com/10useful

SURF THE NET

WWW.DUMMIES.COM

For other technology titles from IDG Books Worldwide, go to
www.idgbooks.com

Not on the Web yet? It's easy to get started with Dummies 101®: The Internet For Windows® 95 or The Internet For Dummies®, 5th Edition, at local retailers everywhere.

IDG BOOKS WORLDWIDE™

Find other ...For Dummies books on these topics:
Business • Career • Databases • Food & Beverage • Games • Gardening • Graphics
Hardware • Health & Fitness • Internet and the World Wide Web • Networking • Office Suites
Operating Systems • Personal Finance • Pets • Programming • Recreation • Sports
Spreadsheets • Teacher Resources • Test Prep • Word Processing

IDG BOOKS WORLDWIDE BOOK REGISTRATION

Register This Book and Win!

We want to hear from you!

Visit **http://my2cents.dummies.com** to register this book and tell us how you liked it!

- ✔ Get entered in our monthly prize giveaway.

- ✔ Give us feedback about this book — tell us what you like best, what you like least, or maybe what you'd like to ask the author and us to change!

- ✔ Let us know any other ...*For Dummies*® topics that interest you.

Your feedback helps us determine what books to publish, tells us what coverage to add as we revise our books, and lets us know whether we're meeting your needs as a ...*For Dummies* reader. You're our most valuable resource, and what you have to say is important to us!

Not on the Web yet? It's easy to get started with *Dummies 101*®: *The Internet For Windows*® *95* or *The Internet For Dummies*, 5th Edition, at local retailers everywhere.

Or let us know what you think by sending us a letter at the following address:

...*For Dummies* Book Registration
Dummies Press
7260 Shadeland Station, Suite 100
Indianapolis, IN 46256-3945
Fax 317-596-5498

BUSINESS AND
GENERAL
REFERENCE
BOOK SERIES
FROM IDG

COMPUTER
BOOK SERIES
FROM IDG